Designing Instructional Text

Designing Instructional Text

James Hartley

University of Keele

Kogan Page, London

NP

Nichols, New York

First edition published in Great Britain and
the United States of America in 1978

This 2nd edition first published in Great
Britain in 1985 by Kogan Page Ltd
120 Pentonville Road, London N1 9JN
Reprinted 1986, 1988

British Library Cataloguing in Publication Data

Hartley, James
    Designing instructional text. — 2nd ed.
    1. Printing, Practical — Make-up 2. Text-books
    I. Title
    686.2′2   Z253.5

    ISBN 0-85038-943-7

This 2nd edition first published in the United
States of America in 1985 by
Nichols Publishing Company
PO Box 96, New York, NY 10024
Reprinted 1986, 1988

Library of Congress Cataloging in Publication Data

Hartley, James Ph.D.
    Designing instructional text.
    Bibliography: p.
    1. Text-books — Authorship. 2. Teaching — Aids and
    devices. 3. Printing, Practical — Style manuals. I. Title.
    LB3045.5.H37   1985   070.5′2   85-3063
    ISBN 0-89397-218-5

Printed and bound in Great Britain by
Dotesios (Printers) Ltd, Bradford-on-Avon, Wiltshire

Contents

Contents

Preface to the second edition

Designing Instructional Text is intended to give some general guidelines for producers of instructional materials. The guidelines are based upon current practice – particularly as employed by typographers – and upon a critical reading of relevant research. This research has increased dramatically in the interval between the first edition (1978) and the second one (1985). The text has been extensively rewritten and expanded accordingly.

The notion of planning is emphasized throughout the text. This is done for two reasons. First, instructional text is usually much more complex in its structure and appearance than is continuous prose – and thus it requires greater care in its design and presentation. Second, technical advances in print and information processing mean that more and more 'non-specialists' are producing instructional materials. Such people require assistance, and planning will help them to be more effective.

The text starts with some basic points about typographic planning (Chapters 1 to 4). The aim here is to assist writers, typographers and printers, and to show how good typographic practice can help the users of instructional text. Chapter 5 demonstrates this point specifically by providing examples of instructional text, first in their original state and then in revised versions following the points made earlier.

The next two chapters (Chapters 6 and 7) focus on writing instructional text. Chapter 6 presents guides to good practice, and Chapter 7 again presents 'before and after' examples, where this time attention is paid both to the typography and to the language of the text.

The second part of the book (Chapters 8 to 14) is concerned with more general issues – such as the role of illustrations and the presentation of quantitative materials. More specialized issues, such as the design of bibliographies and indexes, are considered, and so too are the implications of the material considered so far for the setting of electronic text.

The book concludes with a discussion of the problems of evaluating instructional text (Chapter 15) and an annotated bibliography that also lists British standards and other resources.

Acknowledgements

A number of people have helped in the preparation of *Designing Instructional Text*. Peter Burnhill was responsible for the typographic design and, in addition to Patricia Wright, Jeremy Foster and Paul Lefrere, he advised on certain chapters. John Coleman prepared much of the artwork. Doreen Waters, Margaret Woodward and Dorothy Masters helped Alice Slaney with the major work of typing repeated drafts. I am very grateful to these people and to the many others who helped in one way or another with the production of this text.

James Hartley
February, 1985

Chapter 1

Page-size

In this chapter I consider the importance of selecting the page-size of a book or document before taking decisions about the detailed planning of the work. I discuss the value of choosing a page-size from the range of standard sizes recommended by the International Organization for Standardization.

If readers of this textbook care to take a look at a range of printed materials they will see that they come in many shapes and sizes. Until recently there have been no specific rules or guidelines which would suggest to writers, designers or printers why they should choose one page-size in preference to any other. The research literature on legibility and textbook design offers little help, for page-size is not an issue that features in many textbooks on typographic research. Why then do I choose to open this guide to designing instructional text by discussing page-size?

Many people expect a review of typographic design to begin by considering such issues as typesizes, typefaces, and line-lengths. However, it is important to realize that the choice for each of these variables is already constrained by an earlier decision. Clearly we do not expect to find large typesizes in a pocket dictionary or a single column of print in a daily newspaper. These examples are extreme, but they illustrate the point. The choice of page-size comes first, and this affects the choices that are available for subsequent decisions.

The size of the page determines the size of the overall visual display to the reader. The reader needs to be able to scan and read this display easily – be it large, like a wall chart or a double-page spread, or small, like a pocket dictionary or timetable. Readers need to be able to scan, read, and focus on both gross and fine details. The size of the page constrains the decisions writers and designers must make about these details.

Let us consider, as an example, the choice of page-size for this book *Designing Instructional Text*. I chose the International Standard size A4. This size allows me to display the text as I wish, and as I want the readers to see it. The choice of A4 has allowed me to use a one-third/two-thirds column structure. In the narrower column I have positioned chapter summaries and figure captions. In the wider column I have positioned the body of the text. I have chosen this in preference to a two-column structure with columns of an equal width. My choice allows me to use large illustrations without them cutting across the columns of print: I can position illustrations from the left-hand margin of either the narrow column or the wider column, according to their size.

In addition, having decided on A4, it was possible for me to prepare the typescript and the artwork in such a way that (it is to be hoped) reduced time, effort and even mistakes in the printing of the book. The first draft of this book was prepared in typescript with each line containing a maximum of 75 characters: this length matches the character length of this printed text. Such a procedure allowed me to see where line-endings would fall – a point I wish to consider later.

If I had chosen A5, then the organization of the information on the page, the artwork, and the typing would all have been different.

The choice of an appropriate page-size is not always easy. A number of factors contribute to decisions about which page-size to use. Perhaps the most important one is some knowledge of how the text is going to be used. One limitation of A4 in this respect is that when an A4 textbook is open the double-page spread occupies a large space – and there may not be room for this on everybody's desk. Another limitation is that A4 books require wider shelving. Other positive factors, however, have to be balanced against limitations such as these. In my case I wanted to present a number of illustrations which varied in size, and I did not want to have to reduce the size of this illustrative material to something so small that readers would not be able to appreciate the subtleties of what they were being shown.

Other factors which affect the choice of page-size are such things as the costs of production and marketing, reader preferences, what page-sizes are indeed available and, more generally, the need to conserve resources and avoid waste. In the case of printed texts the most obvious thing that can be wasted is the paper itself. It is for this reason that there is great interest in manufacturing *standard* page-sizes, and the International Organization for Standardization has achieved an intriguing solution to this problem.

Standard page-sizes

The page-sizes that we commonly see are cut from a much larger basic sheet which has been folded several times. The present-day variety in page-sizes results from manufacturers using different sizes for their basic printing sheets and folding them in different ways. If the basic printing sheets were all one standard size, however, and the method of folding them allowed for little if any wastage at the cutting stage, then great economies could be achieved.

The need to rationalize paper sizes has been discussed for a long time in the history of information printing. In 1798, for example, the French government prescribed a standard for official documents based on the proportion of 1:1.41 with a basic printing sheet of one square metre in area. In 1911, Wilhelm Oswald proposed 1:1.414 (that is, $1:\sqrt{2}$) as the 'world format'. In 1922 the German standard, DIN 476, was published. For this standard the ratio of $1:\sqrt{2}$ was retained with a basic printing sheet size of one square metre. The German standard, together with the A, B and C series of sizes, was adopted in 1958 by the International Organization for Standardization (ISO). Today the ISO series is recommended by the 50 or more national standards bodies which together make up the ISO.

The dimensions of the sizes in the ISO A and B series of sizes are set out below. The C series relates to envelope sizes for use with standard-sized documents and need not concern us here. In the United Kingdom the A series is now well known, especially the more commonly used A4 and A5 sizes. The B series, which is rooted in the same principle as the A series, and whose sizes fall in between those of the A series, is not so well known.

ISO series of trimmed paper sizes:

A series		B series	
Designation	Size (mm)	Designation	Size (mm)
A0	841 x 1189	B0	1000 x 1414
A1	594 x 841	B1	707 x 1000
A2	420 x 594	B2	500 x 707
A3	297 x 420	B3	353 x 500
A4	210 x 297	B4	250 x 353
A5	148 x 210	B5	176 x 250
A6	105 x 148	B6	125 x 176
A7	74 x 105	B7	88 x 125
A8	52 x 74	B8	62 x 88
A9	37 x 52	B9	44 x 62
A10	26 x 37	B10	31 x 44

The unifying principle of the ISO-recommended range of sizes is that a rectangle with sides in the ratio of $1:\sqrt{2}$ can be halved or doubled to produce a series of rectangles *each of which will retain the proportions of the original*. A rectangle of any other proportion will generate geometrically similar rectangles only at every other point in the process of halving or doubling (see Figure 1/1).

Figure 1/1
ISO paper sizes

(1) This diagram illustrates the principle of construction and shows that the ratio of the sides of the rectangle is the same as that of the side of a square to its diagonal.

(2) This illustrates the fit between the A and the B series of sizes. For example, B5 falls between A5 and A4, and is geometrically similar.

(3) A rectangle of non-standard proportions. Note that the process of halving generates two geometrically dissimilar series of rectangles.

(4) A rectangle of standard proportions. This case is unique in that halving generates geometrically similar rectangles at each point in the series.

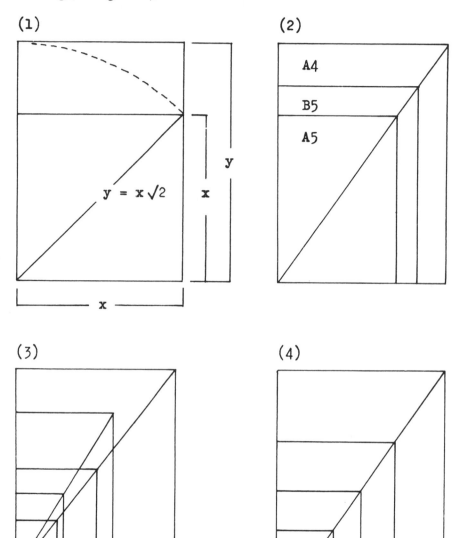

As the pages of a book are made by folding the larger basic sheet in half – once, twice or three times or more – all pages made from a standard size basic sheet will be in the ratio of $1:\sqrt{2}$. Basic sheets which do not conform to the standard bear no rational relationship to one another and do not exhibit the property of geometric similarity when folded to form pages of a book.

Geometrical similarity in format means, among other things, that typeset information which has been prepared for a standard page-size need not necessarily be reset, but simply enlarged or reduced photographically when it is required for use with any other format which complies with the ratio of $1:\sqrt{2}$. Similarly, artwork for diagrams and illustrations, and the blocks or negatives made from such artwork, need not be remade when used in differing contexts, such as the design of wall charts, work cards, or overhead projector transparencies, when the format complies with the standard width-to-depth ratio. In other words, the use of a geometrically similar format helps with the interchange of all of these materials.

One further comment can be made here about the value of standard page-sizes to the design of instructional materials. Until the 1970s most of the early typographical research was confined to studying the legibility of letters and lines of information set in paragraph style. Even at this level of structure, where typesize and line-length are necessarily constrained by the page-size chosen, many research workers ignored the dimensions of the page as a basic parameter in the organization of text. As a consequence typographical research has, until recently, tended to be divorced from practical problems which arise in the planning and use of structured text. Such a situation limits the accumulation of knowledge to 'on-the-job' practice. In my view, the recognition of standard page-sizes by research workers is a necessary condition for further development in the design and evaluation of instructional material which is normally complex in structure.

Summary

1. **The choice of a particular page-size for a particular piece of instructional text is mainly related to the circumstances in which the instructional text is to be used.**

2. **Until now pages have varied widely in size because of the use of different basic printing sheet sizes.**

3. **To rationalize the field, the ISO standard page-sizes should be used.**

4. **Standard page-sizes will lead to an easier interchange of dimensionally compatible units of instructional text – and assist typographic research.**

Chapter 2   Basic planning decisions

In this chapter I discuss the importance of advance planning in the layout of instructional materials and I outline the rationale and use of the typographic reference grid.

If we look at pages of instructional text we can see that the component parts of the information are highly differentiated and varied in character. Unlike a novel, which may consist of little more than lines of text set in paragraph form and an occasional chapter heading, instructional text usually contains a wide variety of components – such as listed information, programmatically developed statements, numbered items, diagrammatic presentations, explanatory notes and pictorial features of many kinds. Typographically, instructional materials are far more complex than novels.

Furthermore, much of this material will not be read continuously. A learner's focus of attention often ranges from one place on the page to somewhere else: to another page, to the instructor, to the task in hand, to the blackboard, to other learners, and, of course, back again to that same place on the page. The spatial arrangement of the text must support this situation by providing a consistent frame of reference within which the learner can move about, leave and return without confusion.

The principal weakness of many instructional materials is a lack of consistency in the positioning of functionally related parts. In textbooks, for example, the relative position of the illustrations and of the text which refers to them frequently changes, both within a page and from page to page. As the book is used, the learner must constantly be asking: 'Where am I supposed to go from here?' (Examples to illustrate this point are presented in Chapter 5.)

This kind of confusion in the sequential organization and the grouping of the parts shows not only a lack of rigour in the initial planning of the pages, but also a weakness in bridging the gap between typographical planning and print production. If one inspects many textbooks it is hard not to come to the conclusion that they are often composed page by page *during* production, on a sort of 'let's put this here' basis. Such a procedure produces inconsistency from page to page, particularly in terms of the spacing and positioning of different components. In the world of building, such a procedure would be equivalent to erecting a house without reference to a formal specification or plan. When it is considered that the cost of producing a book may equal that of erecting a building, then some idea may be gained of the wastage and cost of muddling through in this way. The cost to the person who has to use the material is something which, at present, we do not have the means to measure.

The reference grid

If confusion and waste are to be minimized in the planning and production of instructional materials, then the spacing of the parts must be decided in detail before steps are taken to set in motion the typesetting and the designing of the illustrations. The typographic reference grid is an essential element in planning and in communicating design requirements to the printer.

In a less disciplined approach to print design a sketch is sometimes drawn showing rectangles to indicate blocks of 'text' and the position of illustrations. This may be helpful but, strictly speaking, such a drawing is not a reference grid. As can be seen from Figure 2/1a, the *basic reference grid* is a system of numbered co-ordinates which maps out the information area of the page in identically dimensioned modules of space. This basic grid is the foundation for the drawing of a *master reference grid* (or set of grids) to be used in specifying the particular design requirements of the work in hand (see Figure 2/1b).

Figure 2/1a

Basic reference grid. The grid maps
out the information area of the page.
The information (text, illustrations,
etc) need not fill this area, but
should not extend beyond it.

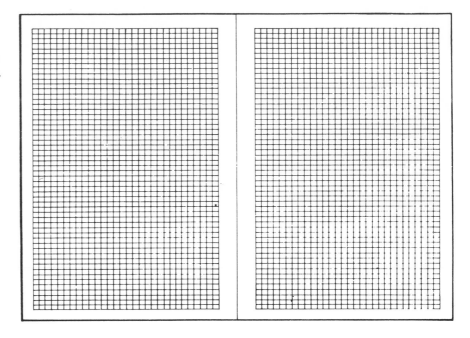

Figure 2/1b

Master reference grid. This grid
specifies the particular dimensional
requirements of the work.

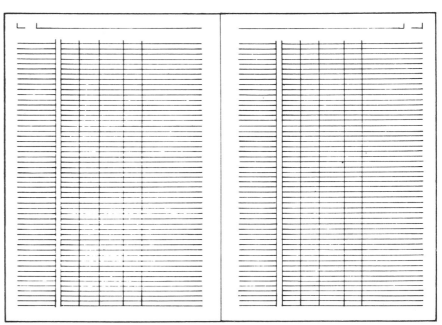

To construct a basic reference grid the designer must decide the width and
depth of the unit or module of the grid. This unit is then used in the
specification of the overall dimensions of the information area of the page,
and of the subdivisions of it. For example, the width of columns, the space
between columns and the amount of space which is to be left before and
after headings and between items of text will be expressed in multiples of the
grid modules, as will the position and the dimensions of the spaces allocated
to the printing of diagrams and illustrations (see Figures 2/1c and 2/1d).

Figure 2/1c

Text and grid combined. This figure shows how the grid and the text relate. Note the widest margin in the 'gutter'. Also note that the side headings fall within the information area, not in the margins as such.

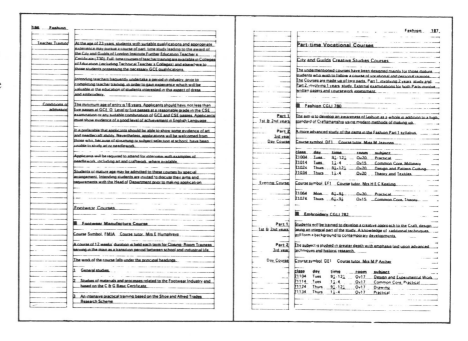

Figure 2/1d

The final printed page. The grid lies invisibly 'behind' the printed image of the text and so provides a reliable frame of reference for the reader which is consistent throughout the work.

Spaces between items are whole multiples of the line-feed dimension and may not be changed. These spaces (one, two or four units) are indicated on the typescript when the copy is marked up for typesetting. Decisions concerning the dimensions of a space should be made by the writer or the designer by reference to the hierarchical construction of the information. No typist or typesetter can be expected to do this at the same time as operating a typewriter or a typesetting machine.

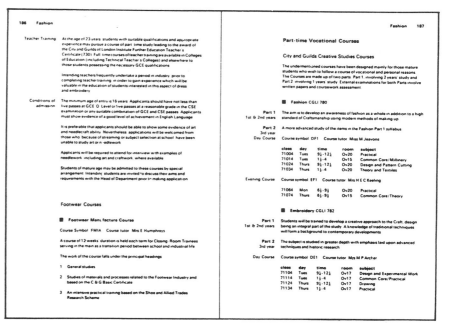

The designer must have information about the system of measurement associated with the method to be used to keyboard the text before the reference grid can be constructed. At present, the art of information processing and printing is such that the unit of measurement associated with character assembly mechanisms may be one of four mutually incompatible systems of measurement: the Anglo-American point system, the Didot point system, the inch, and the metric system. In practice this means that designing may entail the use, side by side, of two or more of these systems. For example: the typist's copy of the author's text may have been produced on an inch-based typewriter, its transformation to typeset form may entail the use of the Anglo-American point system, and the measurement of the page may be expressed in units of the metric system.

Although clearly not conducive to clarity or efficiency in the movement of information from one surface to another, this lack of a unified system of measurement need not prevent us from discussing basic principles.

What determines the vertical dimension of one module or grid space? As can be seen in Figures 2/1c and 2/1d, the depth of the module is identical to the distance measured perpendicularly from the baseline of one line of text to the baseline of an adjacent line. This distance is usually called the 'line-space' and it is equivalent to the line-feed dimension to which the typewriter or type composition system has been set. The choice of this dimension is dependent on the choice of typesize plus an increment of space between the lines of type to ensure legibility. These factors will be discussed in more detail in Chapter 3.

What determines the horizontal dimension of one module of grid space? If the Anglo-American point system of measurement is used in the assembly of the text, the width of the module is normally 12 points. (One point measures approximately 1/72 inch.) If the metric system is used, then some suitable multiple of the typometric unit (0.025 mm) is normally selected – say, 5 mm. Using an inch-based, fixed character-width typewriter, a suitable width for the unit would be a space equivalent to two characters (that is 1/6 inch on a machine producing 12 characters to the inch).

When the vertical and the horizontal dimensions of the grid module have been decided upon, then attention can be turned to the maximum permissible width and depth of the reference grid – namely, the dimensions of the information area, or what is referred to traditionally as the 'type area'.

The information area

The information area can be defined as that part of the page outside of which no printed matter will appear. In some kinds of book design the information area is a sharply defined rectangle of print surrounded by wide margins. In such cases the area devoted to margins may occupy as much as 50 per cent of the page area (see Figure 2/2). This practice stems from the time when books were bought in sheet form to be folded, trimmed and specially bound in leather by the purchaser for inclusion in a private library. In the case of a book published in several sizes, the size of the information area remained constant and it was the width of the margins and the quality of the paper which helped to determine the size and price of the book: the wider the margins, the larger the book and the higher its price.

Figure 2/2

(1) The type area of the traditional private library book may occupy no more than 50 per cent of the area of the page.

(2) In the planning of highly structured information, the space traditionally devoted to margins is used functionally in the spacing of the various parts of the information. In this case the designer will use as much of the page area as possible. At the same time, the printed matter will not be made to pack the information area at the expense of the functional grouping of the parts of the whole achieved through internal spacing. (See Figures 2/1c and 2/1d.)

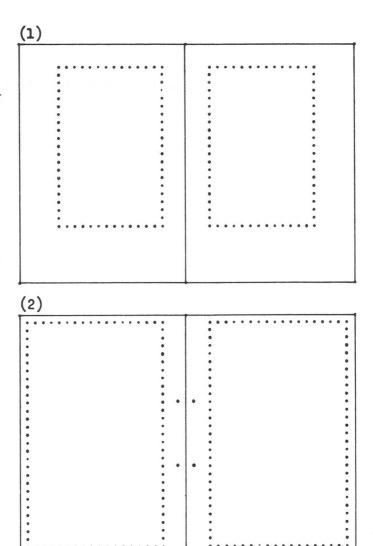

The visual consequences of past commercial and technical practices still tend to influence thinking about the aesthetics of page design. None the less, today's typograpic designer will be more interested in using the space of the page in a manner which is dictated by the structure of the information than in forcing the print to fit rigidly into rectangular blocks.

Generally speaking, at the top, bottom and opening edge of the document, a margin of about 10 mm minimum is necessary for technical reasons associated with the print production process. The fourth margin (the inner or binding edge margin) is a special case. Here, thought should be given to factors which may indicate the need for a wider margin. For example, the printed page may be copied at some time and the copies punched for filing with other material. The binding system itself may involve the punching of pages, or it may be of the kind that causes some part of the edge of the page to be hidden from view. Or the binding system may be such that text or diagrams printed too close to the binding edge may curve inwards and be difficult to read. For these reasons, a margin of about 25 mm is usually necessary at the binding edge of both left- and right-hand pages.

With these constraints in mind we can decide the precise dimensions of the usable area of the page (the information area) measured in whole units of the grid module. The maximum permissible *depth* of the area will be specified in terms of a whole number of grid modules, that is, a whole number of possible lines of text, including such lines as may be required for page numbers, running heads and other points of reference. As regards the maximum permissible *width* of the information area, the typographer's preference will be for a number of grid units which will subdivide readily and which, if necessary, will provide a series of column widths and intercolumn spaces for use with the ISO standard range of page-sizes (see Figure 2/3).

It is important to observe that the overall dimensions of the print area delimit the planning field; they are not intended as an invitation to fill it arbitrarily.

Summary

1. **The printed page should provide a reliable frame of reference from within which the readers can move about, leave and return without confusion.**

2. **Planning pages to this end should be completed in detail before work begins on the typesetting of the text and the designing of the artwork.**

3. **The typographic reference grid is an essential tool in the process of planning instructional materials and for informing typists, illustrators, compositors, and printing machine operators of design and dimensional requirements.**

4. **The dimensions of the grid module must be decided by reference to the system of measurement associated with the character assembly system and the requirements of legibility.**

5. **Once decided, the grid module is the unit used for specifying all linear measurements associated with textual and pictorial components and with the spaces between them.**

6. **The depth of the information area will include lines containing page numbers and similar points of reference.**

7. **The overall width of the information area is determined by having regard for technical and functional problems likely to occur at the margins of the page, and by choosing a number of grid modules which allows for this and which will subdivide readily.**

Figure 2/3

Some of the possible subdivisions of ISO standard pages.

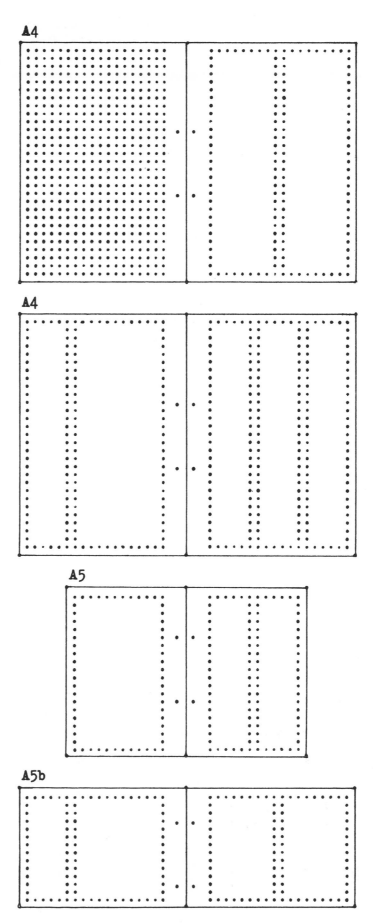

Chapter 3

Typesizes, typefaces and spacing

In this chapter I discuss factors affecting the choice of typesizes and typefaces. I point out that such choices are affected by practical matters: what is available and what should be avoided. The use of italic, bold and capitals for emphasis is discussed, and the chapter concludes with some observations on the printing of numerals and mathematical text.

In Chapter 2 I discussed the typographic reference grid and explained that the depth of each module of the grid is based upon the unit of line-feed chosen for the work and that the width of each module is based upon the chosen typesize. In this chapter I shall discuss further the main factors which determine a typographer's choice of typesize and line-feed dimension.

As we move to consider these more detailed decisions we find an increase in the amount of research on the subject. For example, several researchers have made suggestions concerning typesizes for reading matter and have advised on such related factors as line-length and line-spacing. Tinker (1963) and Watts and Nisbet (1974) provide good summaries.

Unfortunately, however, much of the research in these areas is not very helpful to designers of instructional materials. This is principally because such variables as typesize, line-length and interline space have not been studied in the context of instructional text. Most researchers, for example, have considered typesize in simple typographic settings such as continuous prose. Furthermore they have usually used 'justified' text – that is text which has a straight left- and right-hand edge or margin. In justified text (*un*like this text) the spacing between the words is varied from line to line, and words may be hyphenated in order to form lines of equal length.

Perhaps the most confusing aspect of past research in this field, however, has been the tendency to suggest typesizes without proper regard for the fact that the specified size of a typeface (say 12 point) does *not* refer to the dimensions of the image of the printed characters as seen by the reader. The specified size refers instead to the depth of space required by a line of type when it is set with the minimum line-to-line space: the actual image size may vary within this space.

Figure 3/1, for instance, shows the same phrase printed in one *size* of type but in three type styles. At best, typesize is but a first approximation to image size.

Figure 3/1

The same phrase printed in three styles but one size of type.

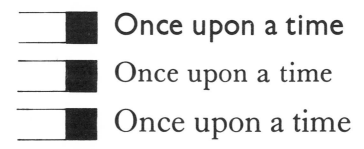

It is not my intention here to recommend typesizes for use in the printing of instructional materials, especially as the specified size of a set of characters can only be a rough approximation to the actual size of the printed image of the letters and the words. However, I would like to outline one approach to the problem of choosing a typesize for a text. At root, this concerns two factors:

1. One needs to choose a maximum permissible line-length which, when related to the typesize, will not obstruct the proper and sensible phrasing of the information; and

2. One needs to consider the relationship between the word spacing and the line-to-line spacing of the information.

Line-length and typesizes

A typographer will search the author's work carefully to look for problems which could arise if too large a typeface is chosen. (For example, if in a child's reading book the maximum permissible length of a line is limited by the typesize to three or four words, then syntactic grouping of the words in lines may be difficult to achieve.) An A5 page, for example, with an information area of, say, 24 x 5 mm modules in width allows for a line-length of nine or ten five-letter words when the printed characters are a little larger than those used for adult reading. Using the same image size, an A4 information area of, say, 36 x 5 mm modules in width will permit a line-length of about 15 words. In brief, the primary dimension to be considered in relation to typesize is the *width* of the character groups and syntactically structured word-strings, not the vertical dimension of a character *per se*. This is shown in Figure 3/2.

Figure 3/2

An increase in typesize affects the length of a phrase, which is sometimes forgotten when an increase in typesize is suggested.

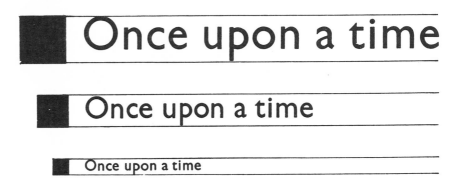

Line-spacing

Line-space is the dimension measured perpendicularly from the baseline of one line of text to the baseline of the next line (see Figure 3/3). Line-space is minimal when it is the same dimension as the typesize. In this minimal state, the interlinear space (the *apparent* space between the lines of words) may appear to be less than the space between the words.

Figure 3/3

This figure shows the relationships between typesize and line-space.
1 base line
2 line space
3 typesize
4 interlinear space (in this case, zero; ie typesize = line-space).

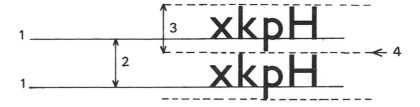

The opening out of lines to create a clear difference between the interlinear gap and the word-spacing is common practice when ease of reading is required. In this way, the danger of optical bridging between lines is reduced. Satisfactory spacing is achieved when the minimum line-space dimension is increased by an amount equivalent to the dimension specified for the word-spacing of the text. In this way, the interlinear gap will never appear to be less than the word-spacing of the text (see Figure 3/4).

Figure 3/4

Top: Type is set 'solid', ie no extra line-spacing.

Bottom: Type is set with extra line-spacing of the same dimension as the word-spacing.

Optimum line-spacing is achieved when the line-space dimension is increased by an amount equivalent to the amount specified for the word-spacing of the text.

Once upon a time
there was a piece
of wood. It was not

Once upon a time there was a piece of wood.
It was not the best wood, but just a common piece,
such as we use in stoves and fireplaces to kindle
a fire and warm our rooms in winter. I can't say
how it happened, but the fact is that one fine day
this piece of wood happened to be in the shop of an

Once upon a time
there was a piece
of wood. It was not

Once upon a time there was a piece of wood.
It was not the best wood, but just a common piece,
such as we use in stoves and fireplaces to kindle
a fire and warm our rooms in winter. I can't say
how it happened, but the fact is that one fine day
this piece of wood happened to be in the shop of an

In the past, when metal type was set by hand, line-spacing would be inserted after the lines had been set. Today, when information is assembled through a keyboard system of one kind or another, line-spacing is included at the same time as the text is keyed. However, lines of space cannot be set systematically unless the keyboard operator is informed by marks on the copy of the precise number of units of line-space required at any given point in the information. The printer, therefore, must be given clear instructions concerning the number of lines of space to leave between items.

Word-spacing

In justified text, all the lines of text are of equal length, and are made so by varying the spacing between the words from line to line and by hyphenating or breaking words at line ends. In structured information, however, word groups may be allowed to vary in length as the sense demands. This allows word-spacing to be of a fixed amount throughout the work (as in this text) and no words need be broken at line ends.

Word-spacing should be large enough to allow the grouping of characters – the word-images – to be clearly differentiated. This is achieved when the width of the word-space is about 25 per cent of the designated typesize. This, traditionally, is the width of the space allowed for the lower-case letter 'i' (see Figure 3/5). On the standard office typewriter, however, where all characters are allocated the same space, word-spacing may be as much as 50 per cent of the minimum line-to-line dimension of the text.

Figure 3/5

This figure shows that the width of spaces between words is that of a lower-case letter 'i'.

Once|upon|a|time

Onceiuponiaitime

Once upon a time

When word-spacing is specified as 25 per cent of the typesize, then the line-to-line dimension – the vertical dimension of the grid module – should be about 1.25 of the typesize. For example, a line-to-line dimension of 5 mm would indicate the use of a typesize no greater than 4 mm in the overall depth of the character images. In this case, the word-spacing would be 1 mm.

It should be remembered that here we are discussing principle. In practice, the dimensions specified must be related to the measurement system which is built into the character composition system. As noted earlier, this could be one of the four measuring systems currently used in the printing industry.

Typefaces

One particular source of confusion to students of textbook design is the bewildering range of typefaces currently available to printers. For example, one encyclopaedia of typefaces lists over 2,350 entries, and Zachrisson (1965) lists 19 typefaces in common use in Western Europe. Watts and Nisbet (1974) provide several illustrations of different typefaces.

Although the emphasis which is frequently placed on letter styles may confuse the student, in practice choice is normally left to the designer, and designers are constrained by what is available to them. For the designer, choosing a typeface really means:

1. Knowing which method of character assembly will be used for the work and ascertaining its performance characteristics;

2. Knowing which character sets are available for use with the system and which are held by the printer;

3. Making sure that the sizes and weights required for the work are available;

4. Making sure that the character set contains not only the commonly used signs but also special characters called for by the author's text, if any; and

5. Assessing the suitability of the design of the characters relative to the need to minimize the chances of image degradation in the printing process.

In printing instructional materials the typefaces to avoid are of two kinds:

1. Those which may confuse the learner by exhibiting idiosyncratic features in the shape of particular characters or in the overall design of the character set; and

2. Those which may readily suffer loss of identity when printing or copying is less than perfect. Factors to be wary of in this latter connection are:
    (a) fine lines which may break down;
    (b) small internal spaces which may fill in;
    (c) strong contrast between thick and thin strokes which may cause a dazzle effect, especially when the print is on very white or glossy paper; and
    (d) letters which appear to touch one another, and which may actually run together if slightly over-linked or under-exposed. (It is worth noting here that photo-lithographic printing has many more points in the stages of print preparation in which image degradation can occur than does the traditional letterpress process. Although this is no argument for using only letterpress, the choice of character style is especially important when the printing is to be by the photo-lithographic method – which is increasingly common in the production of textbooks.)

In general, instructional materials should be printed in characters which are firm in line, open and even in spacing and without idiosyncratic features in their design.

Capital letters

Words printed only in capital letters contain less distinctive information per unit of space than do words set in lower-case characters of the same typesize, so word recognition may be less immediate (see Figure 3/6).

Figure 3/6

The same phrase printed in capital and in lower-case letters.

ONCE UPON A TIME

Once upon a time

WHOLE PARAGRAPHS OF TEXT SET IN CAPITAL LETTERS ARE GENERALLY BELIEVED TO BE MORE DIFFICULT TO READ THAN IS TEXT SET IN NORMAL UPPER- AND LOWER-CASE LETTERS. AS WE SHALL SEE IN CHAPTER 15 THIS FACT IS PARTICULARLY RELEVANT TO THE SETTING OF ELECTRONIC TEXT. THE USE OF STRINGS OF WORDS IN CAPITALS FOR MAIN HEADINGS (OR SMALL CAPITALS FOR SECONDARY HEADINGS) MAY BE SATISFACTORY BECAUSE, NORMALLY, SUCH HEADINGS ARE SURROUNDED BY SPACE WHICH AIDS THEIR PERCEPTION. ON the whole, though, the use of capital letters should be kept to a minimum. Apart from specialized use in mathematical work, capital letters are best reserved for the first letter of a sentence (including headings), and for the first letter of proper nouns.

Writers occasionally use capitalized words as a means of emphasis. This is understandable when handwriting or typewriting offer no method other than capitalization or underlining. However, this change in the appearance of the word-image may confuse the less able reader. Underlining, on the other hand, may cause technical problems. If a change from the norm is really necessary, then the **bold version** of the lower-case letters can provide it without radically changing the geometrical characteristics of the word-image.

It must be remembered, of course, that young readers cannot be expected to know automatically why a change from the norm has taken place. This particularly applies to the printing of individual words in bold or in colour. Furthermore, we need to remember that changes from the norm, whether in letter-style, size, boldness, colour or position, can have no value if they are used excessively.

Italicized letters

Sloping or 'italic' characters were introduced originally into printed books in the sixteenth century as a means of setting more characters to the line, the style of letters being more compressed than the vertically drawn and rounded forms of the normal lower-case character set. Again, it is commonly believed that continuous italic text is harder to read than the more conventional typographic settings. Today, italicized characters are often used in instructional materials as a means of emphasizing a word in the text, or for the titles of books when these appear in the writing of the text or in bibliographic references. In school texts designed for young children, the use of the italicized form is normally unnecessary, except of course in the context of mathematical statements where italicized signs have special significance.

Numerals

The arabic numerals associated with some typefaces assume an up-and-down appearance when set in groups. Numerals of this kind are called non-ranging or 'old style' (see Figure 3/7). For instructional materials, standard or ranging numerals are to be preferred to the non-ranging kind. In mathematical text, numerals which align with one another, both vertically and horizontally, are obviously necessary. Non-ranging numerals may confuse the young reader.

Figure 3/7

Left: Ranging numerals.
Right: Non-ranging numerals.

— **1 2 3 4 5** — 1 2 3 4 5 —
— **6 7 8 9 0** — 6 7 8 9 0 —

Mathematical textbooks and worksheets provide particularly difficult design problems, and require careful specification in advance if spatial consistency is to be maintained throughout the text. It is now becoming the practice for authors to write mathematical text on appropriate grid sheets.

Summary

1. **The main dimension to be considered in choosing typesize is line-length.**

2. **Optimum line-spacing is achieved when the minimum line-to-line dimension is increased by an amount equivalent to the dimension specified for the word-spacing of the text.**

3. **The precise amount of space required between each item of text should be indicated when the copy is marked up for typesetting. Normally, this spacing will be in multiples of line-feed.**

4. **The choice of type style is determined by practical matters – by what is available and by what to avoid.**

5. **Typefaces to avoid are (a) those with idiosyncratic designs, and (b) those which will not withstand degradation when printed and copied.**

6. **The use of capitals, italics, underlining, etc should be used sparingly, and children need to be told what such changes are intended to indicate.**

7. **The use of standard (ranging) numerals is to be preferred in mathematical materials, which should be planned on appropriate grid sheets.**

Chapter 4   Space and structure

In this chapter I discuss further how one can manipulate the vertical and the horizontal dimensions of a piece of text in order to clarify its structure.

So far we have seen that a typographic reference grid is an essential aid to the planning and production of printed text. We have also noted that the vertical dimensions of the grid are determined by units of line-feed. These issues were discussed in more detail in Chapters 2 and 3. In this chapter I focus on how the vertical and horizontal dimensions of the printed matter can be manipulated in order to enhance the clarity of the text.

Comprehension and retrieval

One of the main arguments of this textbook is that what affects most the ease of comprehension and retrieval from printed text is the use that is made of the *space* on a page-size of known dimensions. Although the print is important – and clearly one cannot do without it – the clarity of this print can be enhanced by a rational and consistent use of the 'white space'.

Space plays an important role in clarifying text. It is space that separates the letters from each other. It is space that separates the words from each other. It is space (with punctuation) that separates phrases, clauses, and paragraphs from each other; and it is space (with headings and subheadings) that separates the subsections and the chapters from each other.

There is some evidence, admittedly equivocal, from eye-movement research which suggests that these spatial cues are important aids to understanding text. It is argued, for instance, that with increasing maturity and experience, readers come to rely more heavily on such spatial cues to enhance their reading and search efficiency. It has been shown that the beginning of a line (and not its end) has a marked effect on eye-movement fixations, and that text which starts in an irregular manner (such as poetry or figure captions in some texts) produces more regressive fixations (look backs) than does regularly spaced text.

Many psychologists maintain that consistent spacing helps readers to see redundancies in the text, and thus to read faster; it enables them to see more easily which bits of the text are personally relevant for them; but, most important, consistent spacing aids readers' perception of the structure of the document as a whole and thus it helps them to understand its organization and structure.

Vertical spacing

The spacing of a page can be considered from both a vertical and a horizontal point of view. Let us take vertical spacing first. The argument here is that the structure of complex text can be demonstrated more clearly to the reader by a consistent and planned use of vertical spacing. In effect units of line-feed (vertical space) can be used consistently in such a way as to separate out components of the text – such as sentences, paragraphs, sub and major headings. One simple way of using line-feed in this way is to use it in a proportional system. One can, for example, start each sentence on a new line within a paragraph (*no* extra line-feed); separate paragraphs by *one* extra line-feed unit; separate subheadings from paragraphs by *two* extra lines above and one below; and separate main headings from text by *four* extra lines above and two below. In essence, this is the system used in this textbook except that I have not started new sentences on a new line within paragraphs. This is a procedure that I reserve for more complex text.

Figure 4/1a

A traditionally spaced piece of text.

General

    This section describes the care, maintenance and inspection of insulating rubber blankets. This section is re-issued to delete reference to the KS-13602 cleaner; this has been superseded by the B cleaning fluid (AT-8236).

Description

    An insulating rubber blanket is made of flat, flexible sheets of black rubber. These sheets do not contain either beaded edges or eyelets. The blankets are approximately 36 inches square, 1/10th inch thick and weigh approximately 7lbs. The electrical, weather, and chemical resistance properties of the blanket are very good.
    Rubber stamped on each blanket is a "Return for Test" date. Blankets must be returned for testing by that date to the Western Electric Company - or other authorized agent. The blankets should be returned in rolls (3-1/2 ins. diameter) and wrapped properly so as to avoid damage. A replacement blanket will be made available when a blanket is returned for testing.

Inspection

    Before using a blanket inspect it each time for cracks, cuts, tears or other mechanical damage as follows: ...

What is the effect of such an approach? Figure 4/1a shows a traditionally spaced piece of text, and Figure 4/1b shows a revised version using the system described above. Figure 4/2 shows three settings from more complex text, one piece 'set solid', one opened up with minimal spacing, and one with proportional vertical spacing.

Such proportional systems are effective ways of ensuring consistent vertical spacing between the component parts of a piece of text. Other systems (not proportional, but regular) can be used and, indeed, for more complex text one might wish to introduce indentation or horizontal shifts in the text to convey further substructure. (See later examples in Chapter 5.)

Finally, in this section on vertical spacing, we should note that if the vertical spacing between the components of the text is to be consistent throughout the text, then this leads to the idea that the text should have what is called a *floating baseline*. This means, in contrast to traditional printing practice, that the text does not stop at the same point on every page, irrespective of its content. The stopping point on each page is determined by the content rather than by the need to fill the page.

Figure 4/1b

A revised version of Figure 4/1a.

<u>General</u>

This section describes the care, maintenance and inspection of insulating rubber blankets.
This section is re-issued to delete reference to the KS-13602 cleaner; this has been superseded by the B cleaning fluid (AT-8236).

<u>Description</u>

An insulating rubber blanket is made of flat, flexible sheets of black rubber.
These sheets do not contain either beaded edges or eyelets.
The blankets are approximately 36 inches square, 1/10th inch thick and weigh approximately 7lbs.
The electrical, weather, and chemical resistance properties of the blanket are very good.

Rubber stamped on each blanket is a "Return for Test" date.
Blankets must be returned for testing by that date to the Western Electric Company - or other authorized agent.
The blankets should be returned in rolls (3-1/2 ins. diameter) and wrapped properly so as to avoid damage.
A replacement blanket will be made available when a blanket is returned for testing.

<u>Inspection</u>

Before using a blanket inspect it each time for cracks, cuts, tears or other mechanical damage as follows: ...

Designing Instructional Text has such a floating baseline. The grid specification allows for the depth of the information area to be 62 units of line-feed plus or minus two. This means that one can use an extra line (or two) if a paragraph ends at this point. It means that headings do not appear as the last item on a page, nor do paragraphs end on the top line of the next page. And, unlike traditional printing practice, the internal spacing of the text is not squeezed or expanded in order to make the text fit into a prescribed rectangle.

Figure 4/2

Settings for complex text.

(a) Set solid (ie no spatial cueing).

(b) Minimum spacing introduced to group items hierarchically.

(c) This spacing is now increased proportionately.

These settings form part of a series of systematically worked out layouts for this particular piece of material. (This text is part of the British Standards 3700: Recommendations for the Preparation of Indexes.) The layouts are reproduced here by permission of Sandy Banks and Bert Aureli.

7 Presentation

7.1 Introductory note

An index should be preceded by an introductory note, explaining the indexing decisions which have been made. The note should draw attention to any matter excluded from the index, and to the system of alphabetization chosen. Abbreviations, symbols, variant typography, etc., should also be explained (see 5.1.1.1, 5.1.3, 5.1.4, 5.3, 6.1, 6.2.1.2, 6.2.3.1, 7.2.4.3, 7.3.1).

7.2 Column and entry layout

7.2.1 Columns

It is usually more economical of space to arrange the entries in two or more columns on the page, but this depends on the average length of the entries. If subheadings are run on, the columns should be wide enough for easy legibility.

7.2.2 Indention

Headings, subheadings and subsubheadings should be progressively indented. Run-on continuations should be indented sufficiently to avoid confusion with subheadings.

7.2.3 Entry layout

7.2.3.1 Each subheading should begin on a new line for reasons of clarity, though in long indexes this may be impracticable.

7.2.3.2 For clarity in very long, run-on indexes, subentries may be grouped in paragraphs.

7 Presentation

7.1 Introductory note

An index should be preceded by an introductory note, explaining the indexing decisions which have been made. The note should draw attention to any matter excluded from the index, and to the system of alphabetization chosen. Abbreviations, symbols, variant typography, etc., should also be explained (see 5.1.1.1, 5.1.3, 5.1.4, 5.3, 6.1, 6.2.1.2, 6.2.3.1, 7.2.4.3, 7.3.1).

7.2 Column and entry layout

7.2.1 Columns

It is usually more economical of space to arrange the entries in two or more columns on the page, but this depends on the average length of the entries. If subheadings are run on, the columns should be wide enough for easy legibility.

7.2.2 Indention

Headings, subheadings and subsubheadings should be progressively indented. Run-on continuations should be indented sufficiently to avoid confusion with subheadings.

7.2.3 Entry layout

7.2.3.1 Each subheading should begin on a new line for reasons of clarity, though in long indexes this may be impracticable.

7.2.3.2 For clarity in very long, run-on indexes, subentries may be grouped in paragraphs.

7 Presentation

7.1 Introductory note

An index should be preceded by an introductory note, explaining the indexing decisions which have been made. The note should draw attention to any matter excluded from the index, and to the system of alphabetization chosen. Abbreviations, symbols, variant typography, etc., should also be explained (see 5.1.1.1, 5.1.3, 5.1.4, 5.3, 6.1, 6.2.1.2, 6.2.3.1, 7.2.4.3, 7.3.1).

7.2 Column and entry layout

7.2.1 Columns

It is usually more economical of space to arrange the entries in two or more columns on the page, but this depends on the average length of the entries. If subheadings are run on, the columns should be wide enough for easy legibility.

7.2.2 Indention

Headings, subheadings and subsubheadings should be progressively indented. Run-on continuations should be indented sufficiently to avoid confusion with subheadings.

7.2.3 Entry layout

7.2.3.1 Each subheading should begin on a new line for reasons of clarity, though in long indexes this may be impracticable.

7.2.3.2 For clarity in very long, run-on indexes, subentries may be grouped in paragraphs.

Horizontal spacing

One can consider the horizontal spacing of text in much the same way as we have considered the vertical spacing. That is to say we can look to see how the horizontal spacing can be used to separate and group components of the text, and how one can vary the stopping point of horizontal text in accord with its content rather than by using arbitrary rules about line-lengths.

In traditional printing practice it is conventional for the columns of print to have a straight right- and left-hand edge (see Figure 4/3a). Technically this is called *justified* composition. As we noted in Chapter 3, justification is achieved by varying the spaces between the words and sometimes by using hyphenation. Indeed, in some cases with very narrow columns (eg in newspaper composition), the spaces between the letters forming the words are also varied in order to force the text to fit a given length of line.

A different approach to setting text is to provide a consistent space between each word (see Figure 4/3b). Such a procedure produces *unjustified* composition – as in this textbook. Here there is the same amount of space between each word, and no word-breaks (hyphenation); consequently the text has a ragged right-hand edge.

Experiments have shown that there is little to choose between justified and unjustified composition in terms of legibility, reading speed or comprehension, although there are some indications that unjustified composition might be more helpful for less able readers (be they younger children or older adults). In terms of costs, however, when traditional methods were used rather than computer-based ones, there was an advantage for unjustified composition, and this was particularly so when it came to the resetting of proof corrections (as it was easier to slot them in).

However, it is doubtful whether these experimental studies have considered fully all of the advantages of unjustified composition. One clear advantage of unjustified composition is that one does not have to fill up each line with text: one can consider (as with vertical spacing) where best to end the line.

With unjustified text, for instance, it is possible to specify that no line should end with the first word of a new sentence, or that if the next to the last word on a line is followed by a punctuation mark then this last word could be carried over to the next line. (Compare Figure 4/3b with Figure 4/3c).

Figure 4/3c is in fact based on Bradbury Thompson's design for *The Washburn College Bible*. This Bible is printed throughout in unjustified text, and line-endings are determined by syntactic groupings. *The Washburn College Bible* is actually a *lectern* Bible. It is printed in large type to allow the minister to read it out loud to the congregation, and undoubtedly its typographical format helps the minister in this respect.

Figure 4/3d is an additional suggestion which shows how one can consider the *starting* as well as the *stopping* points in setting text of this kind. Research (with much less poetic text) has shown that readers prefer lists of items to be set out vertically (and possibly indented) rather than to run on in continuous text (see Chapters 6 and 13).

Figure 4/3a

An example of justified text.

Now the sons of Jacob were twelve. The sons
of Leah; Reuben, Jacob's firstborn, and
Simeon, and Levi, and Judah, and Issachar,
and Zebulum. The sons of Rachel; Joseph,
and Benjamin: And the sons of Bilhah, Rachel's
handmaid; Dan, and Naphtali. And the sons of
Zilpah, Leah's handmaid; Gad, and Asher.
These are the sons of Jacob, which were born
to him in Padan-aram.

Figure 4/3b

Unjustified text with consistent
word-spacing.

Now the sons of Jacob were twelve. The sons
of Leah; Reuben, Jacob's firstborn, and
Simeon, and Levi, and Judah, and Issachar,
and Zebulun. The sons of Rachel; Joseph,
and Benjamin: And the sons of Bilhah, Rachel's
handmaid; Dan, and Naphtali. And the sosn of
Zilpah, Leah's handmaid; Gad and Asher.
These are the sons of Jacob, which were born
to him in Padan-aram.

Figure 4/3c

Unjustified text with line-endings
determined by syntactic
considerations.

Now the sons of Jacob were twelve:
The sons of Leah;
Reuben, Jacob's firstborn,
and Simeon, and Levi, and Judah,
and Issachar, and Zebulun:
The sons of Rachel;
Joseph, and Benjamin:
And the sons of Bilhah, Rachel's handmaid;
Dan, and Naphtali:
And the sons of Zilpah, Leah's handmaid;
Gad, and Asher:
These are the sons of Jacob, which were born
to him in Padan-aram.

Figure 4/3d

Unjustified text with listed statements
and syntactic line-endings.

Now the sons of Jacob were twelve:
The sons of Leah;
    Reuben, Jacob's firstborn,
    and Simeon, and Levi, and Judah,
    and Issachar, and Zebulun:
The sons of Rachel;
    Joseph, and Benjamin:
And the sons of Bilhah, Rachel's handmaid;
    Dan, and Naphtali:
And the sons of Zilpah, Leah's handmaid;
    Gad, and Asher:
These are the sons of Jacob, which were born
to him in Padan-aram.

Combining vertical and horizontal spacing

So far I have discussed the vertical and horizontal spacing of text as though they were separate issues – which, of course, they are not. In some texts interrelated decisions need to be taken which will depend upon the nature of the text. If the text consists of nothing but continuous prose, then (on an A4 page) a two-column structure with normal paragraph indentation may be perfectly acceptable. If, however, the text consists of numerous small elements, all of which start on a new line, then indentation to denote new paragraphs can be misleading (see Figure 4/4). It is for reasons such as these that I generally advocate the use of a line-space rather than indentation to denote new paragraphs in instructional text.

Figure 4/4

Indentation is inappropriate for one-sentence paragraphs.

The young of most mammals are born alive, instead of being hatched from eggs.

The young of all mammals are fed with their mother's milk.

All mammals have some hair or fur on their bodies.

All mammals have warm blood.

Theory into practice

The implementation of a systematic use of vertical and horizontal space can cause some difficulties for printers and designers. Some of these difficulties are conceptual or aesthetic: some people seem resolutely opposed to the notion that one can design text by starting from the top left and working downwards – they prefer a centrally balanced presentation.

Other concerns are more practical. Printers have little difficulty in printing unjustified text and in following pre-prepared grids, but it is perhaps asking too much of typesetters to ask them to consider the meaning of each line of text so that they can determine its appropriate stopping point.

There are, however, some techniques which can aid printers in this respect. For example:

1. Texts can be prepared in such a way that the actual number of characters per line corresponds to the line-length to be used by the printer in the setting of the text. In typing the manuscript for this text, for example, we set the line-length to correspond to the width of this section of the grid, ie 75 characters maximum. The printer then followed the manuscript more or less line for line.

2. Authors can prepare their manuscript line for line as they wish, and the manuscript can be photographed. One advantage of preparing camera-ready copy is that it allows authors almost complete control over the preparation of their text.

3. Developments in computer-assisted typesetting will allow one to use grammatical constraints as determinants for line-endings. Figures 4/5a and 4/5b show advances in this respect. Figure 4/5a shows a piece of text set in the standard form: Figure 4/5b is the same text 'chunked' by computer.

Many readers will no doubt prefer the original setting of Figure 4/5a to the computer-based setting of Figure 4/5b – which many see as 'too ragged'. However, computer-aided printing is a rapidly developing field. In my view it will not take a great deal of programming effort to implement the guidelines for spacing advocated in this chapter and to produce more acceptable results.

Summary

1. **The organization of text can be enhanced by its spatial layout.**

2. **Units of line-feed can be used consistently throughout a text to separate and group related parts of the text.**

3. **Similarly, consistent word-spacing can be used as a device for better displaying the structure of text.**

4. **Computer-assisted printing methods can help printers to set texts in the ways suggested in this chapter.**

Figure 4/5a

The original text.

A useful theory of design would combine general principles with specific task requirements. It would also be explicit about the means of doing this, that is, describe precisely how a particular design problem might be solved. Our current work on documentation problems contributes to a design theory of this type. The work is motivated by the following assumption. If we can take a text, create a multitude of rational design variations, evaluate them according to different text and reader skill assumptions and deliver up the best design option, then all of these activities together would constitute a workable theory of design.

Figure 4/5b

Text 'chunked' by computer into meaningful segments. Figure courtesy of NJ Macdonald and LT Frase of Bell Telephone Laboratories.

A useful theory of design
would combine general principles
with specific task requirements.
It would also be explicit about the means of doing this,
that is, describe precisely
how a particular design problem might be solved.
Our current work on documentation problems contributes
to a design theory of this type.
The work is motivated
by the following assumption.
If we can take a text,
create a multitude of rational design variations,
evaluate them according to different text
and reader skill assumptions
and deliver up the best design option,
then all of these activities together
would constitute a workable theory of design.

Chapter 5   Theory into practice (i)

This chapter presents examples of instructional materials in their original state. These examples are criticized in the light of the foregoing discussion, and revised versions are presented.

Example 1

Figure 5/1a shows a page from an introductory primary school geography text published some 30 years ago. In this illustration four factors have caused the structure of the information on the page to be less clear than it might be.

1. The choice of typesize (and thus line-length) works in opposition to the need to phrase the text clearly, line for line. In one place the typesize has had to be changed so that the grouping of the items can be set out properly.

2. The printer has used justified text: this causes variability in the word-spacing and the breaking of words (with hyphens) at the line-ends. Breaking words is not in the best interest of the child's understanding of the word-image.

3. The space between the lines is not used to group the material syntactically. The practice of indenting lines at the start of a statement is not a satisfactory way of indicating the structure of the information clearly.

4. The use of capitals for emphasis is confusing, as is the use of split words.

Figure 5/1b shows a revised version with these considerations in mind.

Figure 5/1a The original layout.

because it is not such a long time ago since we found them.
   Here then are these six continents :—
NORTH   EUROPE.   ASIA.
AMERICA.
SOUTH   AFRICA.   AUSTRALASIA.
AMERICA.
The western pair The middle pair   The eastern pair
   Down in the far south there is a seventh continent.   It is so cold that ice and snow cover it all the time and no one lives there. It is called AN-TARC-TIC-A and the South Pole is in it.
   Then we must have a look at the Oceans. Between Europe and Africa and the Americas is the AT-LAN-TIC OCEAN.
   Between the Americas and Asia-Australasia is the PA-CI-FIC OCEAN.
   Between Australasia and Africa is the INDIAN OCEAN.
   These are the oceans in the middle parts of the earth.   Round the north of the world, in the very cold areas, there is the ARCTIC OCEAN.
   It is mostly frozen up.   The North Pole is in it.   Round the Southern parts of the world, around Antarctica, is the SOUTH-ERN OCEAN.

Figure 5/1b A revised version of Figure 5/1a.

because it is not such a long time ago since we found them.

Here then are these six continents:
North America   **Europe**   **Asia**
South America   **Africa**   **Australasia**
The western pair   The middle pair   The eastern pair

Down in the far south is a seventh continent.
It is so cold that ice and snow cover it all the time
and no one lives there.
It is called **Antarctica.**
The South Pole is in it.

Then we must have a look at the Oceans.

Between Europe and Africa and the Americas
is the **Atlantic Ocean.**

Between the Americas and Asia-Australasia
is the **Pacific Ocean.**

Between Australasia and Africa
is the **Indian Ocean.**

These are the oceans in the middle parts of the Earth.

Round the north of the world, in the very cold areas,
is the **Arctic Ocean.**
It is mostly frozen up. The North Pole is in it.

Round the southern parts of the world, around Antarctica,
is the **Southern Ocean.**

Example 2

Figure 5/2a shows a page from a junior science textbook. The principal weakness of this page is the unsystematic way in which the illustrations, and the text which refers to them, have been arranged. Muddle of this kind is common in primary school textbooks. It is principally due to a lack of rigour in planning and specification before beginning the work of typesetting and illustrating. Figure 5/2b shows a revised version.

Figure 5/2a

AIR PRESSURE

How do you know that air is all around you?

Can you see it?   No.

Can you smell it?   No, only when it carries some substance which has a smell.

Can you feel it?   Yes, when the wind blows.

Has air any weight?   Yes. The weight of air, or " air pressure ", is approximately 15 lb. per square inch on *every* surface in *every* direction.

Does air push upwards as well as downwards?   Yes.

EXPERIMENT TO SHOW THAT AIR CAN SUPPORT A COLUMN OF WATER

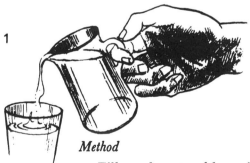

Air can support things. You can carry out an experiment to show that air can support a column of water. You will need a tumbler, a piece of cardboard and water.

Method

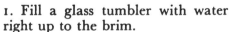

1. Fill a glass tumbler with water right up to the brim.

2. Slide a piece of cardboard over the top of the glass so that it touches the water. Do not allow any bubbles of air to creep in.

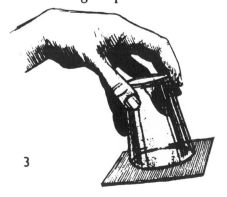

3. Turn the tumbler upside down holding the card against the glass. Take your hand away from the card. If you do this carefully, the water will remain in the tumbler. It will not fall out because it is supported by the air pressure below.

Figure 5/2b

Air pressure

How do you know that air is all around you?

Can you see it?
No.

Can you smell it?
No, only when it carries some substance which has a smell.

Can you feel it?
Yes, when the wind blows.

Has air weight?
Yes.
The weight of air, or 'air pressure' is approximately fifteen pounds per square inch on every surface and in every direction.

Experiment to show that air can support a column of water.

Air can support things.

You can carry out an experiment to show that air can support a column of water.

You will need:
a tumbler; a piece of cardboard; water.

20

Method

1 Fill a tumbler with water up to the brim.

2 Slide a piece of card over the top of the glass so that it touches the water.
Do not allow air bubbles to creep in.

3 Turn the tumbler upside down holding the card against the glass.
Take your hand away from the card.
If you do this carefully, the water will remain in the tumbler.
It will not fall out because it is supported by the air pressure below.

21

Example 3

Figure 5/3a shows a page from a primary mathematics textbook. The criticisms that can be made of this page are as follows:

1. In this example the children first have to work *across* from left to right, doing 5(a), (b), (c), etc and then 6(a), (b), (c), etc. They then work *down*, doing 1, 2, 3, etc.

2. In answering questions 5 and 6 the children are likely to have difficulty in knowing exactly where they have got to because the sub-items (a) and (b) are not clearly differentiated from each other by space.

3. The question indicators (1, 2, 3, etc) are embedded in the text, and items 1, 2, 3, etc are not differentiated from each other by appropriate spacing.

Figure 5/3a

---

5 How much change should you get from 50p when you spend:
(**a**) 40p, (**b**) 20p, (**c**) 30p, (**d**) 10p, (**e**) 45p, (**f**) 25p, (**g**) 42p, (**h**) 38p, (**i**) 27p, (**j**) 34p, (**k**) 22p, (**l**) 17p?

1 Tom had 5p. He spent $3\frac{1}{2}$p. How much had he left?
2 Jim had 10p. He spent $4\frac{1}{2}$p. How much had he left?
3 Jean had 25p. She spent 6p on chocolate and 5p on sweets.
(**a**) How much did she spend?
(**b**) How much had she left?
4 John had 20p. He spent 9p on comics and 2p on sweets.
(**a**) How much did he spend?
(**b**) How much had he left?

6 How much change should you get from 100p when you spend:
(**a**) 50p, (**b**) 70p, (**c**) 80p, (**d**) 40p, (**e**) 95p, (**f**) 75p, (**g**) 45p, (**h**) 25p, (**i**) 42p, (**j**) 38p, (**k**) 58p, (**l**) 16p?

5 Anne went out with 30p. She spent 8p on cakes and 7p on lemonade.
(**a**) How much did she spend?
(**b**) How much had she left?
6 Shirley had 50p. She bought sweets for 12p and biscuits for 9p.
(**a**) How much did she spend?
(**b**) How much had she left?

Figure 5/3b shows the same information redesigned with these points in mind.

Figure 5/3b

---

5   How much change should you get from 50p when you spend:

a	40p	e	45p	i	27p
b	20p	f	25p	j	34p
c	30p	g	42p	k	22p
d	10p	h	38p	l	17p

6   How much change should you get from 100p when you spend:

a	50p	e	95p	i	42p
b	70p	f	75p	j	38p
c	80p	g	45p	k	58p
d	40p	h	25p	l	16p

1   Tom had 5p. He spent $3\frac{1}{2}$p. How much had he left?

2   Jim had 10p. He spent $4\frac{1}{2}$p. How much had he left?

3   Jean had 25p. She spent 6p on chocolate and 5p on sweets.
   a   How much did she spend?
   b   How much had she left?

4   John had 20p. He spent 9p on comics and 2p on sweets.
   a   How much did he spend?
   b   How much had he left?

5   Anne went out with 30p. She spent 8p on cakes and 7p on lemonade.
   a   How much did she spend?
   b   How much had she left?

6   Shirley had 50p. She bought sweets for 12p and biscuits for 9p.
   a   How much did she spend?
   b   How much had she left?

Example 4

Figure 5/4a

The front side of the original leaflet. (Reproduced with permission of the Editors of the *Bulletin of the British Psychological Society*.)

Please Note

IGNORE THE LONDON ADDRESS

In an attempt to keep costs (and subscriptions) down we will be using 'old' stationery for some time.

All communications should be addressed to:
The British Psychological Society
St. Andrews House
48 Princes Road East
Leicester LE1 7DR

There is an ex-directory phone number for Members; it is:
(05333) 549593

PLEASE AMEND YOUR ADDRESS BOOK NOW!

SUBSCRIPTION RATES 1977

The subscriptions for 1977 are the same as 1976 as below:

	CASH or CHEQUE	BANKERS ORDER
SUBSCRIBER, GRADUATE, ASSOCIATE, FELLOW (RULES 28 and 28A)	£18.00	£16.00
GRADUATE WITH THREE YEAR CONCESSION (RULE 28B)	£14.00	£12.00
OVERSEAS MEMBER (RULE 28C)	£12.00	N/A
STUDENT SUBSCRIBER (RULE 30)	£ 4.00	£ 4.00

JOURNALS 1977

Prices per volume (all issues for 1977) for journals are shown below. Please use this box to order your journals.

TITLE	RETAIL	MEMBERS, AFFILIATES & SUBSCRIBERS	STUDENT SUBSCRIBERS	WANT	PAYMENT ENCLOSED
Br. J. Psychol.	£20.00	£ 4.00	£ 2.00		
Br. J. med. Psychol.	£16.00	£ 4.00	£ 2.00		
Br. J. soc. clin. Psychol.	£19.00	£ 4.00	£ 2.00		
Br. J. math. statist. Psychol.	£15.00	£ 4.00	£ 2.00		
J. Occup. Psychol.	£13.00	£ 4.00	£ 2.00		
Br. J. educ. Psychol.	£ 6.00	£ 4.00	£ 2.00		
Q. Jl exp. Psychol.		£ 9.40	£ 9.40		
Aust. J. Psychol.		£ 4.00	£ 2.00		

JOURNALS TOTAL £ _____

Notes over +SUBSCRIPTION (IF S.O. LAPSED) £ _____

TOTAL VALUE REMITTED £ _____

A single cheque or standing order may be sent PROVIDING the breakdown of amounts is clearly shown.

Some criticisms of this form (Figure 5/4a) are as follows:

1. Visually, this document is chaotic. This is caused by the centred arrangement of the text, the haphazard use of space, and typefaces of ill-considered size and weight. It is not clear which information is the most important.

2. The first thing that hits the eye is the instruction to ignore the London address. What is intended is 'Note the new address'!

3. The heading 'Subscription Rates, 1977' (the most important heading, one might think) is in a smaller typesize than the instruction to amend one's address book, and it has less space between it and the remaining text. This reduces impact.

4. The heading 'Journals 1977' is in a larger typesize, has more space, and thus seems to be the focal point of the form.

5. The form's designer forgot to include space for the respondent's name and address. This caused horrendous problems at the BPS office.

Figure 5/4b

Page 3 of the revision of Figure 5/4a.

```
SUBSCRIPTIONS 1977 (Please tick appropriate box)

   ▱  FELLOW                       (£18.00 Cash : £16.00 Bankers Order)
   ▱  ASSOCIATE                    (£18.00 Cash : £16.00 Bankers Order)
   ▱  SUBSCRIBER                   (£18.00 Cash : £16.00 Bankers Order)
   ▱  GRADUATE                     (£18.00 Cash : £16.00 Bankers Order)
   ▱  GRADUATE WITH
      THREE YEARS CONCESSION       (£14.00 Cash : £12.00 Bankers Order)
   ▱  STUDENT SUBSCRIBER           (£ 4.00 Cash : £ 4.00 Bankers Order)
   ▱  OVERSEAS MEMBER              (£12.00 Cash)

                                    Payment (if sending cash)  _____

JOURNALS 1977
Prices per volume (all issues for 1977) for journals are shown below.
Please order here which journals you require.

                                          Members
                                          Affiliates      Student
Require                      Retail       & Subscribers   Subscribers
   ▱  Br. J. Psychol.        £20.00       £4.00           £2.00        _____
   ▱  Br. J. med. Psychol.   £16.00       £4.00           £2.00        _____
   ▱  Br. J. soc. clin.
      Psychol.               £19.00       £4.00           £2.00        _____
   ▱  Br. J. math. statist.
      Psychol.               £15.00       £4.00           £2.00        _____
   ▱  J. Occup. Psychol.     £13.00       £4.00           £2.00        _____
   ▱  Br. J. educ. Psychol.  £ 6.00       £4.00           £2.00        _____
   ▱  Q. Jl. exp. Psychol.                £9.40           £9.40        _____
   ▱  Aust. J. Psychol.                   £4.00           £2.00        _____

                              Journal total(if sending cash)  _____

   GRAND TOTAL (if sending cash for both subscription and journals)  _____

NAME  _____
         (block capitals, please)

Address  _____

         _____

         _____


Membership No. (if known)  _____

                                             See notes overleaf.
```

Figure 5/4b shows a typescript version of part of a revision to this leaflet. An A4 page folded in half was used to give four A5-size pages. The text was re-arranged as follows:

Page 1. Heading (British Psychological Society: Subscriptions and Journal prices, 1977).
Page 2. Procedures for payment.
Page 3. Subscription rates, journal rates, name and address (this page is arranged so that all things to be completed are on one page, and it is detachable if necessary).
Page 4. Notes.

Note: In this typescript example capital letters are used, whereas in print bold lower-case letters would be preferable.

Example 5

Figure 5/5a

The first page of the original pamphlet sent out by the British Psychological Society. (Reproduced with permission of the Editors of the *Bulletin of the British Psychological Society*.)

THE BRITISH PSYCHOLOGICAL SOCIETY

(Incorporated by Royal Charter)

NOTICE IS HEREBY GIVEN that a Special General Meeting of the Society with be held in the Small Meeting House, Friends House, Euston Road, London NW1 on Saturday 26 October 1974 at 10.30 o'clock in the forenoon, when the following business will be transacted.
(1) To consider, and if thought fit, to approve the following SPECIAL RESOLUTIONS subject to obtaining the formal approval of the Privy Council:

A. That the Statutes of the Society be amended in the manner following, namely, by deleting the existing Statutes 4 and 8 and substituting the following new Statutes:

4. GRADUATE MEMBERS

(1) All persons who were elected Graduate Members of the old Institution and all persons who are elected as hereinafter provided shall be Graduate Members.

(2) A candidate for election as a Graduate Memeber:

  (a) shall satisfy the Council that he has one of the following qualifications and such higher qualifications as may be provided in the Rules: —

    (i) a university degree for which psychology has been taken as a main subject;

    or

    (ii) a postgraduate qualification in psychology awarded by an authority recognised by the Council;

    or

    (iii) such other qualification in psychology as the Council shall accept as not less than the foregoing;

    or

  (b) shall pass to the satisfaction of the Council such of the Society's examinations as may be required by the Rules.

(3) The Council may elect such eligible candidates to be Graduate Members as it thinks fit.

8. SUBSCRIBERS

(1) All persons who were elected Subscribers of the old Institution and who are elected as hereinafter provided shall be Subscribers.

(2) No technical qualification shall be required of a candidate for election as a Subscriber.

(3) A Subscriber shall be proposed in accordance with the provisions of the Rules.

Figure 5/5a shows an extract from a complex piece of prose, the clarity of which is not helped by its original typography. The original four-page document in fact contains seven levels of text. On this page there are six levels: there is a main item of business; Special Resolution A is part of this; Statute 4 is part of Resolution A; Statute 4 has three parts; part 2 has subsections (a) and (b); and subsection (a) has parts (i), (ii) and (iii).

Such a text is difficult – if not impossible – to read if, as in this figure, the spatial organization of the text is completely at variance with the sense.

Figure 5/5b

The British Psychological Society

(Incorporated by Royal Charter)

Notice is hereby given that a Special General Meeting of the Society will be held in the Small Meeting House, Friends House, Euston Road, London NW1 on Saturday 26 October 1974 at 10.30 o'clock in the forenoon, when the following business will be transacted.

1st item of business

To consider, if thought fit, to approve the following Special Resolutions subject to obtaining the formal approval of the Privy Council: (These Special Resolutions are identical with those approved in principle at the Society's Annual General Meeting held in Bangor on 6 April,1974, with the exception of Statute 15 (see below) in which maximum permitted subscriptions have been reduced.)

Resolution A

That the Statutes of the Society be amended in the manner following, namely, by deleting the existing Statutes 4 and 8 and substituting the following new Statutes:

Statute 4: Graduate Members

(1) All persons who were elected Graduate Members of the old Institution and all persons who are elected as hereinafter provided shall be Graduate Members.

(2) A candidate for election as a Graduate Member:

(a) shall satisfy the Council that he has one of the following qualifications and such higher qualifications as may be provided in the rules:-

(i) a university degree for which psychology has been taken as a main subject;

or

(ii) a postgraduate qualification in psychology awarded by an authority recognised by Council;

Figure 5/5b shows a respaced typed equivalent (reduced in size) where the hierarchical nature of the document has been clarified by the rational use of vertical and horizontal spacing.

Example 6

In a study of hospital drug labelling systems Ian Dennis (1975) found:

- A lack of standardization, both between hospitals and within the various classes of preparation used by individual hospitals;

- Poor organization of information: little consistency in the order and terminology of the information, and wide variation in the positioning of the elements of the labels;

- Large type used for short names and small or condensed type used for long names irrespective of whether the kind of information being conveyed was the same or not; and

- Centred and justified typography which, together with a heavy use of capitals and a haphazard mixing of type-styles and typesizes, made the labels difficult to read (see Figures 5/6a and 5/6b).

Figures 5/6a and 5/6b

These figures show designs of labels used in London hospitals.

```
PHARMACY DEPARTMENT
THE LONDON HOSPITAL E.1.

        STOCK
      KAOLIN
         and
     MORPHINE
      MIXTURE
       B.N.F. '68
ADULT DOSE UNIT: 10 ml
   SHAKE THE BOTTLE

BATCH:
```

```
St. Bartholomew's Hospital, E.C.1

       SHAKE THE BOTTLE

KAOLIN AND MORPHINE
     MIXTURE, B.P.C.

DOSE:- 10 to 20ml., DILUTED WITH WATER
```

Dennis, in his report, describes how he and his colleagues set about designing:

- A standardized range of label sizes and positionings;

- A set of basic conventions governing the placing, spacing and grouping of information, and the grading of its importance;

- A restricted range of permissible typefaces;

- A minimum range of typesizes; and

- A consistent positioning of labels in relation to the side and front of the bottle and other containers.

Figure 5/6c

This figure shows a redesigned label. (These figures are reproduced with permission of Ian Dennis.)

**Kaolin
and
Morphine
Mixture**

**Kaolin and
Morphine
Mixture
BNF 68**

Adult dose unit: 10ml

**Shake the bottle
Do not use after**

Stock: ward

**Group Pharmacy
The London Hospital E1 1BB**

A study comparing the effectiveness of the new labels with the original ones was carried out by Dennis. This study showed that nurses made fewer errors locating drugs labelled in the new manner.

Chapter 6

Writing instructional text

This chapter discusses briefly the process of writing, and offers guidelines for writing instructional text. The advantages and limitations of computer-aided writing are considered.

There has been a resurgence of interest in the topic of writing. Most current work is concerned with how children learn to write but there has also been an interest in how adults produce instructional text.

Felker (1980) has published a useful description of the processes involved in producing this kind of material. He distinguishes between three stages: pre-design, design and post-design.

The *pre-design* stage is concerned with planning. It is concerned with making decisions about the scope and purpose of the document. The writer needs to know who the document is for, how it is likely to be used, what constraints will operate in its use, and what constraints will operate on him or her as writer of the document.

The *design* stage is concerned with producing the document. It involves writing the appropriate text, organizing it clearly, and presenting it in a clear and simple language with appropriate illustrative materials.

The *post-design* stage is concerned with editing the document, with testing it with users and with revising it on the basis of the results obtained. The aim of the post-design stage is to improve the document – so editing, testing and rewriting are all positive procedures.

Although this chapter focuses on the design stage of writing, this does not mean that the pre- and post-design stages are not important.

Writing is a complex activity or skill. Like all skills, writing is made up of subcomponents which have to be put together in such a way that guarantees smooth performance. Many of these subcomponents are organized hierarchically and some have priority over others but, even during the writing of a single sentence, the writer shifts attention from one subcomponent to another. Thus the following issues competed for my attention while I was writing the first draft of this present paragraph:
- Who is going to read this chapter?
- How should it be organized?
- Which points should I put first in this paragraph?
- Have I made this point clearly?
- Should I rewrite this bit?
- Is my handwriting clear enough so my secretary can read it?
- Are my deletions and insertions easy for my secretary to follow?

In addition, I noted that when writing the second draft of the paragraph above I stopped at least six times in order to read it through, to alter the sequences within sentences, and to produce a list instead of a long final sentence. No doubt, by the time this paragraph appears in print I will have altered it several times.

My procedure for writing generally involves a first version in long-hand, a second revised version in long-hand, a typescript version which is then revised, and a further typescript which is mildly modified to form the final text. I also find it helpful to leave a period of at least 24 hours between versions. There are variations on this general process, mainly depending upon what I am writing about and whom I am writing for. My processes seem quite normal if one can judge from the relevant research literature on academic writing. Some writers draft and redraft much more than this and some much less.

The advent of wordprocessing is likely to have a profound effect on writers like myself. Wordprocessing is particularly suited to text that has a complex organizational framework, detailed technical aspects, and a frequent need for updating. Writers who have changed from typewriters to wordprocessors (usually) have favourable reactions. Such writers find it easier to focus on composition, and to edit afterwards: this, they say, allows them more time for thinking.

Guidelines for writing instructional text

In this section of the chapter I have drawn together some guidelines on writing from the more technical research literature. The purpose of these guidelines is to give suggestions which readers can consider and use as they think fit when they are preparing instructional text. The aim is to indicate the kind of choices available and the possible effects of making particular choices. Specific circumstances will necessitate more detailed consideration, and this may mean that a particular suggestion will not always be appropriate. Certainly, in writing this chapter, I have noticed that I have often gone against my own guidelines. None the less I believe that being aware of my own suggestions has resulted in a better text.

Organizing text

There are a number of features of text which help readers find their way about it. The design of some of these devices (eg contents pages and indexes) will be discussed in a later chapter, and we have already discussed some of the typographic tools of the trade in this respect (eg the use of italics, bold, and capitals). Here I propose to make a few remarks about titles, summaries, headings and sequencing text.

Titles Titles seem to contain the fewest words possible to describe the content of a text – and sometimes these are supplemented with a subtitle. Such succinct descriptions help to focus attention and expectations, and studies have shown that titles affect the readers' perception and interpretation of ambiguous text. However, it is to be hoped that instructional text will not be ambiguous. One would hardly expect titles to have much effect on the comprehension of instructional text – although they may aid later recall of what the text was about. Unfortunately, I know of no research on typographic variables connected with the setting of titles (eg typesizes, typefaces, weights, etc) and none on the more interesting problems of using different title formats (eg statements, questions, quotations).

Summaries Summaries in text have several possible positions and roles. *Beginning* summaries can tell readers what the text is about, they can help readers decide whether or not they want to read it, and they can help readers who do read it to organize what it is that they are reading. *Interim* summaries can summarize the argument so far, and indicate what is to come. *End* summaries can list or review the main points made, and thus aid the later recall of important points in the text.

There has been some research on the effects of including summaries, and on their position (before or after the text). Mark Trueman and I carried out a series of five experiments using a short (1,000 words) semi-technical text with the same summary placed either before or after it. In four of the five experiments the summaries aided the recall of the text, and this was particularly so for summary-related (and hence important) material. With university students the end summary seemed more efficient, but summaries in either position were equally effective with secondary level schoolchildren.

Summaries can be typeset in many different ways – in medium, bold or italic, in large or small type, boxed in, etc. There is no research to my knowledge on the effect of such typographic variables in this context.

Headings

Headings may be written in the form of questions, statements or (like here) with one- or two-word labels. Headings may be placed in the margin (as here) or in the text (as in the other chapters).

In a series of experiments Mark Trueman and I investigated the role of different kinds of heading (questions versus statements) and their position (marginal versus embedded) with secondary schoolchildren. We concluded that headings aided search, recall and retrieval but that the position and the kinds of heading used had no significant effects with the texts we used. More studies still need to be carried out which manipulate factors such as:
- the nature of the text (technical versus semi-literary);
- the frequency of headings; and
- the typographic denotation of headings at different levels.

Questions

Some of our earlier research suggested that headings in the form of questions were particularly suitable for less able readers, but our more recent (better designed) studies failed to confirm this. None the less it might be important to consider headings in this form for certain texts.

Questions, of course, may be interspersed in the text itself – or presented in a list at the end of a chapter in the form of exercises. Factual questions, interspersed in a passage *before* paragraphs of relevant material, often lead to specific learning. Similar questions interspersed in a passage, but given *after* the relevant content, sometimes lead to more general learning as well.

Sequencing

Apart from work with programmed instruction and work with the design of forms there has been little research on the sequencing of sentences or paragraphs in instructional text. Work with programmed instruction suggests that violations in natural sequences provide little difficulty for most readers but work with forms (see Chapter 12) suggests just the opposite. Here natural sequencing seems best. However, just what is a 'natural' sequence? Posner and Strike (1978) contrast 17 different ways to show that sequencing is not a simple matter.

There are some situations, however, where we might all agree that the sequence used is unhelpful. Take, for example, this odd sequence of instructions for using a ladies' electric razor:
1. To gain access to the heads for cleaning, press the button on the side of the appliance (see Fig. 4).
2. To remove the razor from its packaging . . .

Certainly it seems easier to follow a sequence when events match the temporal order in which they occur. *Compare* 'Before the machine is switched on, the lid must be closed and the powder placed within its compartment' *with* 'The powder must be placed in its compartment and the lid closed before the machine is switched on'.

Sequencing lists

It is fairly common in instructional writing to find a sentence such as this:
Five devices which aid the reader are (i) skeleton outlines for each chapter, (ii) headings in the text, (iii) a glossary for new technical terms,

(iv) a summary, and (v) a comprehensive subject and author index. Research suggests that readers prefer text which has such lists or numbered sequences spaced out and separated, rather than run-on in continuous text. My example would be better thus:

Five devices which aid the reader are:
  (i) skeleton outlines for each chapter;
  (ii) headings in the text;
  (iii) a glossary for new technical terms;
  (iv) a summary, and
  (v) a comprehensive subject and author index.

This example also shows, however, how the use of the Roman numbering system can affect the layout: Arabic numbers – or letters of the alphabet – might be preferable. Another choice is the use of 'bullets' – thus:

Five devices which aid the reader are:
  • skeleton outlines for each chapter;
  • headings in the text;
  • a glossary for new technical terms;
  • a summary, and
  • a comprehensive subject and author index.

Signalling

Another way of making text organization more explicit is to use 'signals'. Signals have been defined as 'non-content words that serve to emphasize the conceptual structure or organization of the passage'. Words and phrases such as *however*, *but*, or *on the other hand*, signal to the reader that some form of *comparison* is to be made. Similarly, words and phrases such as *firstly*, *secondly*, *three reasons for this are . . ., a better example, however, would be . . .*, signal the *structure of the argument* (and comparisons with subsections). Likewise words and phrases such as *therefore*, *as a result*, *so that*, *in order to*, *because*, signal *causal* relationships.

If authors do not provide such signals then the readers are left to infer such relationships for themselves and this may be harder for younger or less able readers. Typographic cues can be used to enhance signalling by printing such words in italic or bold print.

Typographic cueing

If new technical terms are essential, then it is helpful to print them in italic or bold type, or to underline them in typescript when they are first introduced into the text. (Some authors also provide a running glossary in the margin.) Surprisingly enough, there has been virtually no research on italic as a cueing device, although the use of underlining, bold face, and capitals has attracted some attention. The little research that has been done on typographic cueing suggests that:
  • too many cues can be confusing;
  • simple cueing often has little effect unless the reader is told in advance why and how certain things have been cued; and
  • spatial cues are as important, if not more so, than typographic ones in presenting list-like materials (see Chapter 13).

Text factors

Paragraph length

Few researchers have commented on the effects of paragraph lengths. It would seem, other things being equal, that short well-spaced paragraphs make a text look easier to read.

Sentence length

Long sentences – such as this one – are difficult to understand because they often contain a number of subordinate clauses which, because of their parenthetical nature, make it difficult for readers to bear all of their points in mind and, in addition, because there are so many of them, make it difficult for readers to remember the first part of the sentence when they are reading the last part. Long sentences overload the memory system: short sentences do not.

I once wrote 'As a rule of thumb, sentences less than 20 words long are probably fine. Sentences 20 to 30 words long are probably satisfactory. Sentences 30 to 40 words long are suspect, and sentences containing over 40 words will amost certainly benefit from rewriting.' Perceptive readers will notice that many of my sentences contain more than 30 words – but at least they have been scrutinized!

Word length

Like long sentences long words also cause difficulty. It is easier to understand short familiar words than technical terms which mean the same thing. If, for example, you wanted to sell *thixotropic* paint, you would probably do better to call it *non-drip*! One author on style quotes a letter writer in *The Times* who asked a government department how to obtain a book. He was 'authorized to acquire the work in question by purchasing it through the ordinary trade channels' – in other words 'to buy it'. Concrete words and phrases are shorter and clearer than abstract ones.

Clarifying text

Generally speaking, text is usually easier to understand when:

1. Writers produce few sentences containing more than two subordinate clauses. The more subordinate clauses or modifying statements there are, the more difficult it is to understand a sentence. Consider, for example, the problems posed for an anxious student by this examination rubric: 'Alternative C: Answer four questions including at least one from at least two sections (1-5).'

2. Writers use the active rather than the passive voice. Compare the active form, 'We found that the engineers had a significantly higher interocular transfer index than did the chemists' with the passive form, 'For the engineers, as compared with the chemists, a significantly higher interocular transfer index was found'.

3. Writers use positive terms (eg, more than, heavier than, thicker than) rather than negative ones (eg, less than, lighter than, thinner than).

4. Writers avoid negatives, especially double or treble ones. Negatives can often be confusing. I once saw, for example, a label fixed to a machine in a school workshop which read, 'This machine is dangerous: it is not to be used only by the teacher'. Harold Evans provides another example. Compare 'The figures provide no indication that competition would have produced higher costs' with 'The figures provide no indication that costs would have not been lower if competition had not been restricted'. Negative qualifications *can* be used, however, for particular emphasis and for correcting misconceptions. Double negatives in imperatives (eg, 'Do not . . . unless . . .') are sometimes easier to understand than single ones.

**Text
difficulty**

There are many readability formulas that quantify and predict the difficulty of prose text. These formulas typically combine two main measures: average sentence-length and average word-length (usually considered in terms of the number of syllables). Thus, the longer the sentences and the more complex the vocabulary, the more difficult the text.

Two examples of readability formulas follow: one more complex than the other.
The formula to calculate Flesch's Reading Ease Score is:

$$RE = 206.835 - 0.846 \, w - 1.015 \, s$$

where w = number of syllables per 100 words
s = average number of words per sentence.
The higher the RE score, the easier the text.

Table 6/1 shows the relationship between RE, difficulty and suggested reading ages. To save effort and calculation Table 6/2 can be used.

Table 6/1 Flesch 'Reading Ease' scores, text difficulty,
and predicted reading ages.

RE value	Description of style	Required reading skill
90-100	Very easy	5th grade*
80- 90	Easy	6th grade
70- 80	Fairly easy	7th grade
60- 70	Standard	8-9th grade
50- 60	Fairly difficult	10-12th grade
30- 50	Difficult	13-16th grade
0- 30	Very difficult	College graduate

* To obtain a British equivalent it is conventional to add five, so a fifth-grade pupil is 10 years old. Note, however, British schoolchildren have one extra year's schooling compared with Americans. A fifth-grade pupil has completed four years of schooling in the USA, whereas a 10-year-old pupil has completed five years in the UK.

A more simple readability formula is provided by Gunning. He suggests the following procedures:
- Take a sample of 100 words;
- Calculate the average number of words per sentence;
- Count the number of words with three or more syllables;
- Add the average number of words per sentence to the total number of words with three or more syllables; and
- Multiply the result by 0.4.

The result is the (American) reading grade level: you need to add five to obtain an equivalent British reading age.

Formulas such as these have obvious limitations. Some short sentences are difficult to understand (eg God is grace). Some long words, because of their frequent use, are quite familiar (eg communication). Word, sentence, and paragraph order are not taken into account, and neither are the effects of other aids such as illustrations, headings, numbering systems, and typographical layout.

None the less, despite these and other difficulties, readability formulas can be useful tools for comparing the relative difficulty of pieces of text. It is of interest to note, for example, that the predicted reading ease level for the first

Table 6/2
A table for calculating the reading difficulty of text based on the Flesch formula. Each cell gives the reading age in years.
(Table reproduced with permission of Aubrey Nicholls.)

Average Number of Syllables Per 100 Words

Average Number of Words Per Sentence	105	110	115	120	125	130	135	140	145	150	155	160	165	170	175	180	185	190	195
8	9	9	9	10	10	11	11	12	12	12	13 14	13 14	15 17	15 17	15 17	18 21	18 21	18 21	18 21
10	9	9	10	10	10	11	11	12	12	13 14	13 14	13 14	15 17	15 17	18 21	18 21	18 21	18 21	18 21
12	9	9	10	10	11	11	12	12	12	13 14	13 14	15 17	15 17	15 17	18 21	18 21	18 21	18 21	
14	9	10	10	10	11	11	12	12	13 14	13 14	13 14	15 17	15 17	18 21	18 21	18 21	18 21	18 21	
16	9	10	10	11	11	11	12	12	13 14	13 14	15 17	15 17	15 17	18 21	18 21	18 21	18 21		
18	10	10	10	11	11	12	12	13 14	13 14	13 14	15 17	15 17	18 21	18 21	18 21	18 21	18 21		
20	10	10	11	11	11	12	12	13 14	13 14	15 17	15 17	15 17	18 21	18 21	18 21	18 21			
22	10	10	11	11	12	12	13 14	13 14	13 14	15 17	15 17	18 21	18 21	18 21	18 21	18 21			
24	10	11	11	11	12	12	13 14	13 14	15 17	15 17	15 17	18 21	18 21	18 21	18 21				
26	10	11	11	12	12	12	13 14	13 14	15 17	15 17	18 21	18 21	18 21	18 21	18 21				
28	11	11	11	12	12	13 14	13 14	15 17	15 17	15 17	18 21	18 21	18 21	18 21					
30	11	11	12	12	12	13 14	13 14	15 17	15 17	18 21	18 21	18 21	18 21	18 21					
32	11	11	12	12	13 14	13 14	15 17	15 17	15 17	18 21	18 21	18 21	18 21	18 21					
34	11	12	12	12	13 14	13 14	15 17	15 17	18 21	18 21	18 21	18 21	18 21						
36	11	12	12	13 14	13 14	15 17	15 17	15 17	18 21	18 21	18 21	18 21	18 21						
38	12	12	12	13 14	13 14	15 17	15 17	18 21	18 21	18 21	18 21	18 21							
40	12	12	13 14	13 14	13 14	15 17	15 17	18 21	18 21	18 21	18 21	18 21							

College or above

paragraph of Chapter 1 in this textbook is 'fairly difficult', whereas in the original edition it was 'difficult'. I am pleased by such gains since I have developed these guidelines for this second edition. Other comparison studies have shown advantages for more readable text in
- scientific papers
- school textbooks
- correspondence materials
- examination questions
- job aids
- medical instructions
- insurance policies
- legal documents.

Table 6/3 illustrates the effects of clarifying sentences upon examination results.

Table 6/3

The percentage of correct responses to original and revised multiple-choice questions asked in a pre-O level chemistry examination given to approximately 6,000 pupils. Data from Johnstone and Cassels (1978) and reproduced with permission.

Original questions	% correct	Revised questions	% correct
Which one of the following requires a non-aqueous solvent to dissolve it? A Salt B Sugar C Sodium nitrate D Sulphur	34	Which one of the following requires a liquid other than water to dissolve it? A Salt B Sugar C Sodium nitrate D Sulphur	49
An element has only three isotopes of mass numbers 14, 16 and 17. Which one of the following could *not* be the atomic weight of the element? A 14.2 B 15.4 C 16.3 D 17.1	50	An element has only three isotopes of mass numbers 14, 16, 17. Which one of the following could be the atomic weight of the element? A 11.7 B 13.9 C 15.1 D 17.2	62
The atomic weight of chlorine is usually quoted as 35.5. It is not a whole number despite the fact that protons and neutrons have very closely integral atomic weights because A Ions are present B Impurities are present C Unequal numbers of protons and neutrons are present D Isotopes are present	66	The atomic weight of chlorine is 35.5. Why is it not a whole number? A Ions are present B Impurities are present C Unequal numbers of protons are present D Isotopes are present	78

Difficult short sentences

It does not necessarily follow, of course, that passages written in short sentences and short words will always be better understood. Chapanis (1965) provides excellent examples of short pieces of text that are difficult to understand. The one I like best is the notice that reads

PLEASE
WALK UP ONE FLOOR
WALK DOWN TWO FLOORS
FOR IMPROVED ELEVATOR SERVICE

People interpret the notice as meaning 'to get on the elevator I must either walk up one floor, or go down two floors', or even 'to get on the elevator I must first walk up one floor and then down two floors'. When they have done this they find the same notice confronting them! What this notice means, in effect, is 'Please, don't use the elevator if you are only going a short distance'. Chapanis' article is well worth studying. It is abundantly illustrated with short sentences that are hard to understand and (in some cases) potentially lethal.

Ambiguities

Many short (and many long) sentences can turn out to be ambiguous. Consider 'Then roll up the three additional blankets and place them inside the first blanket in the canister'. Does this sentence mean that each blanket should be rolled inside the other, or that three rolled blankets should be placed side by side and a fourth one wrapped around them? (An illustration would clarify this ambiguity.)

Ambiguities, or at least difficulties, often result from the use of abbreviations or acronyms (strings of capital letters which form words, eg PLATO). I once counted 20 such acronyms in a two-page text distributed by our computer centre. The meanings of acronyms may be familiar to the writer but they need to be explained to the reader. Furthermore, readers easily forget what an author's abbreviations stand for.

Clarifying numbers

When presenting numerical data in text, prose descriptions often seem more comfortable than actual numbers. Everyday words that act as rough quantifiers, eg 'nearly half the group', seem adequate for most purposes and are handled with reasonable consistency by most people.

Research has suggested that the following phrases can be used with confidence:

Numerical value to be conveyed	Suitable phrases
above 85%	almost all of . . .
60-75%	rather more than half of . . .
40-50%	nearly half of . . .
15-35%	a part of . . .
under 10%	a very small part of . . .

None the less, it may be better (or at least clearer for the reader) if more exact verbal equivalents of numbers are given. For example:

Numerical value to be conveyed	Suitable phrases
100%	all of . . .
75%	three-quarters of . . .
50%	half of . . .
25%	a quarter of . . .
0%	none of . . .

Verbal descriptions of probabilities are also more comfortable for most people than actual probability statements. People are less consistent, however, in their interpretations of verbal descriptions of probability than they are in their interpretations of verbal descriptions of quantity. If precision is required, actual quantities can be given with a verbal quantifier. For example, one can say 'nearly half the group – 43 per cent – said . . .' or 'There was a distinct chance ($p < 0.06$) that . . .'.

Reference numbers

Paragraphing in text is often aided by the use of numbering systems. Such systems can be used to organize information in many different ways, eg Section 1, 2, 3, or 1.01, 1.02, 1.03, etc.

There has been little, if any, research on the effectiveness of such systems. Most people undoubtedly feel that they are valuable – particularly for reference purposes. But such systems can be abused and they can lead to extraordinary confusion.

Figure 6/1 was provided by Waller to give an illuminating example. He comments with regard to this material (taken from an Open University correspondence text) that such a chaotic use of numbering reflects a general confusion about their purpose.

Figure 6/1

An example of a text with multiple numbering systems (page 10 of S100, Unit 26, © The Open University Press).

26.1.2   A modern coastal environment

The idea of interpreting the past in terms of the present sounds extremely simple, but there are many practical difficulties. An insight into the extent of these can be gained by considering a present-day environment from a geological point of view.

> So, you should now read the section in Chapter 13 of *Understanding the Earth* entitled 'environmental analysis — the beach' (pp. 180-5).

When you read this section, examine Figure 14 in Appendix 3 (p. 34), which summarizes information on the sediments and faunas of a modern beach. Plate A and TV programme 26 are about this area. *Make sure you have examined Figure 14 thoroughly and have read pp. 180-5 of* Understanding the Earth *given above before viewing the television programme.* The post-broadcast notes will refer you to Appendix 3 which describes a 'geological model' of this stretch of coast and summarizes the sequence of 'rocks in the making' in this environment.

Waller concludes his article on numbering systems with the following five guidelines for educational texts:

- Use numbers mainly for reference. Chapter, page and figure numbers are almost always perfectly adequate for continuous prose texts.

- Consider incorporating figure numbers, exercise numbers, and so on in the chapter numbering systems, particularly when there are too few figures for easy location or when too many different systems would cause confusion.

- Use arabic, not roman, numerals.

- Place the numbers near the fore-edge of the book so that it is easy to see them when flicking through.

- If in-text numbering has to be used, place the numbers in the margin rather than within the column.

Footnotes   To Waller's guidelines I would add one more: avoid the use of footnotes. Most footnotes can be incorporated in the text and excess material may be placed in an appendix – where it can be read by the interested reader. Footnotes cause irritation to typists and to printers, and many publishers expressly forbid them. Certainly footnotes are often irritating to the reader because they break up the reading flow[1] and because they seem so irresistible.[2]

Computer aids to writing

Several computer programs have been developed to help writers produce both technical and conventional text. Most of these programs are designed to be run after the text has been written in order to analyse it and to make suggestions for improvement. In the future, however, we may expect such programs to run concurrently with the writing.

One typical suite of programs is 'The Writer's Workbench' which has been developed at Bell Laboratories in the USA. The number of programs available is currently being expanded but Table 6/4 lists some of them.

In 1984 I published a report of how useful these programs had been to me in revising a particular article. I compared the suggestions made by nine colleagues in this respect with the suggestions made by the computer.

The human and the computer aids to writing differed in two main ways. My colleagues were more variable than the computer programs: different colleagues picked on different things to comment on. None made comments in all of the (14) categories of comments that I derived in the enquiry. The computer programs were more thorough and more consistent than my colleagues – but this was over a narrower range of (six) categories. The programs picked up every misspelling, they drew attention to every sentence that was over 30 words long, they indicated that I had missed out a bracket, and they provided me with 85 suggestions concerning better wording! Thus

---

[1] by bringing you down here and making you find your way back
[2] See what I mean?

the computer programs were excellent at doing the donkey work of editing: my colleagues excelled at using their knowledge to point out inconsistencies, errors of fact, and to suggest better examples.

Some of the computer programs that I did not use in my study were those that gave the first and last sentence of each paragraph, or those that printed out just the headings. Such programs would clearly be of value with complex documents for checking on their organization and structure.

Table 6/4
A sample of computer programs available in 'The Writer's Workbench' system developed at Bell Telephone Laboratories.

Programs which indicate:
- spelling errors
- punctuation errors
- word repetitions
- split infinitives
- use of passives
- use of nominalizations
- use of abstract words
- acronyms
- long sentences
- sexist phrases
- awkward choices of words/phrases (with suggested improvements)

Programs which give:
- parts of speech for each word
- readability scores
- average length of sentences
- number of sentence types (simple, complex, compound, compound-complex)
- comparison figures on details such as these for other 'model' technical texts

Programs which:
- summarize the content – by listing headings
- summarize the content – by giving the first and last sentence of each paragraph
- segment the lines of the text according to line-length requirements and syntactic rules

Other programs can display text graphically. By allocating a certain fraction of line-length for each word it is possible to draw up 'pictures' of paragraphs, with each sentence drawn as a line, punctuated as in the original. Such graphs display at a glance whether some sentences are inordinately long or look confusingly punctuated.

The use of computer programs to aid writing is increasing in our primary and secondary schools. The idea here is that just as the typewriter relieves the writer of thinking about the subgoal of producing legible text, so the computer releases the writer from thinking about other subgoals of transcription when writing. Composition becomes enjoyable when it is so easy to edit words, sentences and paragraphs. In addition, there is less fear of failure when the notion disappears that one has to produce a 'neat' handwritten copy the first or second time around.

Summary

1. Writing is a complex skill. Skills are made up of subroutines, all of which are learned, appropriately connected and integrated through practice.

2. The use of summaries, headings, questions and lists helps to organize and sequence text. The use of short sentences and simple vocabulary (generally) makes text easier to read.

3. Computer-aided writing programs suggest how authors might improve the clarity of text. Such programs help authors with the technical details of writing but, at the moment, they do not help a great deal with decisions concerning content.

Chapter 7   Theory into practice (ii)

This chapter presents some more examples of instructional materials in their original state. The examples are criticized in terms of their typography and their text. Revised versions are presented.

Example 1

Figure 7/1a shows part of the instructions for fault-finding in an American telephone system. Figure 7/1b shows that these instructions are easier to follow:

- when some parts of the text are rewritten;

- when each sentence starts on a new line;

- when sub-units are separated by half a line space; and

- when the GO TO instruction is positioned consistently in the text.

Figure 7/1a

```
STEP 5. Place a call to another person.  If you reach the
        other person, GO TO STEP 6.  If you continue to hear
        dial tone after you dial and the telephone has a rotary
        dial, GO TO STEP 18.  If you continue to hear dial
        tone after you dial and the telephone has a push
        button dial, verify that you have Touch Tone Service.
        (You can do this by calling the Telephone Company
        Business Office.)  If you do have Touch Tone Service
        on your line, GO TO STEP 18.  If you do not have
        Touch Tone Service, you will only be able to answer
        calls with this telephone.
```

Figure 7/1b

```
5. Place a call to another person.
   If you reach the other person . . . . . Go to Step 6

   If you continue to hear the dial
   tone, and your phone has a
   circling dial . . . . . . . . . . . . . Go to Step 18

   If you continue to hear the dial
   tone, and your phone has a
   push-button dial, find out
   if you have Touch Tone Service.
   (You can do this by calling
   the Telephone Company Business
   Office with another phone.)
   If you have Touch Tone Service . . . . . Go to Step 18

   If you do not have Touch Tone
   Service this phone can only
   receive calls.
```

Example 2

Figure 7/2a shows the first page of a four-page document. The problems with this page (as I see them) are:

- the setting of the paragraph numbers;

- the confusion between paragraph numbers and numbers in the text (see 2.01);

- the use of justified text; and

- the use of technical terms, long sentences and passive instructions.

Figure 7/2b shows the same text revised with these considerations in mind.

Figure 7/2a

INSULATING GLOVES

1. GENERAL

1.01 This section covers the description, care and maintenance of insulating gloves provided for the protection of workmen against electric shock, and the precautions to be followed in their use.

1.02 This section has been reissued to include the D and E Insulating Gloves.

2. TYPES OF INSULATING GLOVES

2.01 All types of insulating gloves are of the gauntlet type and are made in four sizes: 9-1/2, 10, 11 and 12. The size indicates the approximate number of inches around the glove, measured midway between the thumb and finger crotches. The length of each glove, measured from the tip of the second finger to the outer edge of the gauntlet, is approximately 14 inches.

2.02 There are various kinds of insulating gloves. The original ones were just called Insulating Gloves. After that B, C, D and E Insulating Gloves were developed. As described below, the D Glove replaced the original Insulating Gloves and the E glove replaced the B and C Gloves.

2.03 **Insulating Gloves** are thick enough to eliminate the need for protector gloves and are intended for use without them. These gloves have been superseded by the D Insulating Gloves.

Figure 7/2b

INSULATING GLOVES

1.0   General

1.1   This section describes how to care for
and maintain the insulating gloves
that will protect you from electric shocks.

1.2   The section has been revised to include
the D and E Insulating Gloves.

2.0   Types of Insulating Gloves

2.1   All insulating gloves are made
in the gauntlet style.
There are four sizes: 9½, 10, 11, 12.
The size indicates the approximate number
of inches around the glove across the palm.
Each glove is about 14 inches long
from the bottom of the gauntlet to the top
of the second finger.

2.2   There are various kinds of insulating gloves.
The first kind were originally just called
Insulating Gloves.
After that the B, C, D and E Insulating Gloves
were developed.
As described below, the D Glove replaced the
original insulating gloves, and the E glove
replaced the B and C gloves.

2.3   So **Insulating Gloves** have now been replaced
by D Insulating Gloves.
(Insulating Gloves could be worn without
protector gloves.)

Example 3

Figure 7/3a shows a page from a science worksheet written for secondary schoolchildren. This example suffers from poor spatial organization and confusing text. Figure 7/3b provides a suggested revision.

Figure 7/3a

```
                                                    GUIDE
                                                    SHEET  PN4(1)
"MATERIALS AND STRUCTURE"

TIME: About 4 weeks                      NAME .........................

This GUIDE SHEET will be very important to you during your study of NUFFIELD
PHYSICS PART 4, UNIT 1, and should be firmly fastened into the front of your
file. This GUIDE SHEET tells you the order of doing your work.
Where you see (O) against a piece of work, this means that you must see your
teacher before starting that piece of work.
Where you see (M) against a piece of work this means that you must have that
piece of work marked.
Where you see (T) against a piece of work this means that you must carry out
that piece of work with your teacher.
Where you are told to read a section from a book etc, this means that you first
of all read the section, then read it again preparing a written summary which is
then placed in your file.
STAGE           ITEM                                               MARK
  1.     WORK SHEET 1                    (M)
  2.     Read Chapter 4 "The New Science of Strong Materials". A brief look at
         "Materials" - Longmans Physics Topics, would also be useful.
  3.     PROJECT SHEET 1                 (M)
  4.     Discussion 1  "Choice of material"               (T)
  5.     TEST SHEET 1                    (M)
  6.     Read "Materials and their uses"
  7.     Read "Amount of substance, the mole concept, and its use in solving
         problems". Nuffield Advanced Chemistry Section A Chapter 1. (O)
  8.     TEST SHEET 2                    (M)
  9.     WORK SHEET 2
 10.     Slide 1.16  (Arrange visit to Leicester University)
 11.     WORK SHEET 3
 12.     TEST SHEET 3                    (M)
 13.     WORK SHEET 4                    (M)
 14.     Read Pages 11-19 "Elementary Science of metals"
 15.     Watch film loops "X-ray diffraction 1 & 2"
 16.     PROJECT SHEET 2
 17.     Read "The start of X-ray analysis" Nuffield Chemistry background
         booklet.
 18.     WORK SHEET 5
 19.     Visit Physics Dept Leicester University. X-ray diffraction apparatus.
         Write a report of the visit.
 20.     Slides 1.1 and 1.3.
 21.     Watch film loops "Diffraction of monochromatic X-rays by a powder
         specimen" and "Determination of wavelength of X-rays using a
         diffraction grating".
 22.     TEST SHEET 4                    (M)
```

Figure 7/3b

Name ....

Guide Sheet PN4(1)

Time: about 4 weeks

MATERIALS AND STRUCTURE

This Guide Sheet will be very important to you during your study of
Nuffield Physics, Part 4, Unit 1.
It should be fastened firmly into the front of your file.

This Guide Sheet tells you the order of doing your work.
M means that you must have that piece of work marked.
R means first of all read the section, then read it again preparing a
   written summary for your file.
T means that you must carry out that piece of work with your teacher.
O means that you must see your teacher before starting that piece
   of work.

Stage		What to do	Mark obtained
1.	M	Worksheet 1	
2.	R	Read Chapter 4 "The New Science of Strong Materials". A brief look at "Materials" - Longmans Physics Topics, would also be useful.	
3.	M	Project Sheet 1	
4.	T	Discussion 1. Choice of material.	
5.	M	TEST SHEET 1	
6.	R	Read "Materials and their uses".	
7.	R & O	Read "Amount of substance, the mole concept, and its use in solving problems. Nuffield Advanced Chemistry Section A Chapter 1.	

Example 4

Figure 7/4a shows part of a fire notice currently on display at the University of Keele. A number of criticisms can be made of this notice:

- The language of the poster is unnecessarily abstract: to say that 'It is of utmost importance that persons in a building which is on fire should be given warning' is not action-oriented.

- The sequence of the instructions is a little odd. Telling people to tackle the fire when they have left the building is nonsense.

- The spacing of the text leaves much to be desired.

Figure 7/4b shows a version of the notice revised with these three points in mind.

Figure 7/4a

ON DISCOVERING FIRE

1. <u>Always raise the Alarm at once</u>

    It is of utmost importance that persons in a building which is on fire should be given warning. Use the fire alarm where there is one. Operating the fire alarm does not call the fire brigade so:-

2. <u>Always call the Fire Brigade at once, PO 9-999 or PAX 888</u>

    By Post Office telephone dial 9-999.   If this is not possible use the Internal telephone and dial 888 (Porters Office, Keele Hall) or 508 (Porters Office, Chancellors Building).   Give the correct address, which is:-

        Keele University

        .... Block

        .... Hall/Building

Make certain your message is understood.

3. <u>Always evacuate the Building at once on hearing the alarm</u>

    a. Senior staff present must take charge.

    b. Close windows and doors.

    c. Alert occupants of adjacent and opposite rooms.

    d. Leave the building by nearest available door. Close doors as you go.

    e. Assemble at .... for roll-call.

4. <u>Tackle a Fire</u>

    Only after the preceding actions have been completed. Only if there is no personal risk.

Figure 7/4b

<u>If you hear the fire alarm:</u>

<u>Evacuate the building immediately</u>

- Close all the doors and windows

- Alert anyone in nearby rooms

- Leave the building by the nearest door available

- Close all doors as you go

- Assemble for a roll-call at ....

(Senior staff must take charge)

<u>If you discover fire:</u>

<u>Raise the alarm immediately</u>

- Alert all the people in the building

- Set off the fire alarm, if possible

- Then:

<u>Call the Fire Brigade</u>   P.O. 9-999 or PAX 888 or PAX 508

- Use a black GPO phone if possible

- If not, use a grey Internal PAX phone

- Give the correct address, which is:

  KEELE UNIVERSITY

  .... HALL

  .... BLOCK

- Make sure your message is understood

<u>Tackle the fire</u>

- Only if you have done the above, and

- Only if there is no personal risk

Example 5

Figure 7/5a shows the original instructions from a leaflet provided by an international airline. Figure 7/5b shows a revised version where both the layout and the text have been changed. Both texts could be improved by the addition of illustrative materials.

Figure 7/5a

IMPORTANT INFORMATION FOR OUR PASSENGERS

Even though you may be an experienced air traveler, there are certain features of this airplane with which you may not be familiar.

AUTOMATIC OXYGEN SYSTEM

The higher altitudes at which this aircraft operates require the prompt use of the automatic oxygen system in case of any sudden change in cabin pressure. Should a decompression occur, oxygen masks will drop down. Take nearest mask and promptly place over nose and mouth. BREATHE NORMALLY (NO SMOKING PLACE).

SEAT BELTS

Even if the "SEAT BELT" sign is turned off in flight, it is recommended that you keep your seat belt fastened, whenever you are in your seat.

FLOTATION SEAT CUSHIONS

The cushion on which you are sitting is designed to keep you afloat. In the event of a water landing, grasp the cushion at the rear, pull it forward and take it with you.

EMERGENCY EXITS

There are nine exits provided for your use. The chart below will show you the one closest to your seat. The exits over the wings are removable windows. For easy access to the window, push seat back ahead of the window forward. The two exits at each end of the cabin are doors equipped with fast operating evacuation slides. There is also a door in the rear of passenger cabin. REAR CABIN EXIT (STAIR). (If usable, will be opened by a crew member.)

Figure 7/5b

IMPORTANT!

This aircraft has special safety features.

Read this card carefully.

AUTOMATIC OXYGEN

If, during the flight, there is a sudden change
in cabin pressure, oxygen masks will drop down
automatically.
If this happens
    - take the nearest mask
    - put it quickly over your nose and mouth
    - breathe normally
    - put out all cigarettes.

SEAT BELTS

We suggest that you keep your seat belt
fastened when you are seated - even when the
SEAT BELT sign is turned off.

FLOATING SEAT CUSHIONS

Your seat cushion will keep you afloat if we
make an emergency landing in the sea.
Get hold of the cushion at the back, pull it
forward, and take it with you.

EMERGENCY EXITS

There are nine emergency exits.

The chart on the back of this card shows
the exit nearest to your seat.

The two exit doors at the end of the cabin
are fitted with chutes for sliding down.

To get out over the wings you have to
take out the windows.
To make this easier, put the seat-back down
when you are trying to get to the window.

The door at the back of the cabin is labelled
REAR CABIN EXIT (STAIR).
This door will be opened by a crew member.

Example 6

Figure 7/6a shows an extract from an instructional manual whose clarity is not helped by its layout. Such small typesizes and compressed materials do not help when a trainee is supposed to move to and from an instructional manual to operate equipment.

Figure 7/6b shows a revised version of just a small part of this first page.

Figure 7/6a

Introduction

The balance is a very sensitive piece of precision laboratory equipment, designed to give accurate readings over long periods of time. Due to the danger of damage to some components, particularly the knife edges and their seatings, it is not practicable to transport the balance in the fully operational condition; therefore, some setting-up is necessary after delivery. Although the procedure is straightforward and is fully descirbed in these instructions, it cannot be too strongly emphasised that the operation requires the services of a competent mechanic.

Also, only those adjustments listed should be made.

DO NOT ATTEMPT TO CARRY OUT ANY OTHER ADJUSTMENT OR SETTING.

In case of difficulty, contact your supplier, agent, or E.L.E. Service Department, who will be pleased to advise and assist.

Setting-up

N.B.   Operations numbered 2 to 23 inclusive apply to balances sent "Export packed". On "Home Packed" balances, operations numbered 10, 11, 12, 13, 14, 16 and 17 will have been carried out by E.L.E. prior to despatch. Balances will be clearly marked as follows:

"Home Packed"

"Export Packed"

1.   Place the balance on a level surface and adjust the feet (Items 1) for non-rocking. It is not necessary for the balance to be precisely horizontal.

2.   Remove weight pan cover and scoop. (Items 2 & 3).

3.   Remove any packing underneath the weight pan support (Item 4) and scoop support (Item 5).

4.   Undo the two screws (Items 6) holding the weight pan and scoop supports, and remove these items (4 & 5). At this stage undo the screws (Items 7) and determine which of the end pillars (Items 8 & 28) has the lead trimming weight/s. This should be noted for possible future reference under "Adjustment" (paragraph 19).

5.   Undo the three retaining screws (Items 9) and remove the front fan housing (Item 10).

6.   Unhook the ranging spring (Item 11) at both ends, and remove. A pair of long-nosed pliers will be needed for this.

N.B.

It is essential that great care is taken of this component, and over-stretching (indicated by gaps between the coils in the free state) will render it impossible to correctly set the balance.

7.   Detach the stirrup (on L.H. lower end of the ribbon, Item 12), from bracket (Item 13).

8.   Undo and remove the three hexagon headed screws (Items 14) situated near the outer rim of the underside of the top cover (Item 15). Two screws at front, and one at rear.

9.   Lift the entire upper assembly from the base.

10.   Remove string or other restraint holding the beam assembly (Item 16) onto its seatings.

11.   Remove the rubber cushions from the six knife-edged seatings (Item 17) as follows, for each seating:-

   a.   Remove one screw (Item 18) holding retaining cap (Item 19) and **loosen** the remaining screws.
It is important that the retaining caps are not completely removed, due to the danger of reassembling the cap onto a different seating. This must be avoided, since the cap carries an individually adjusted screw which controls the end float of the pivots.

It is interesting to note here that the redesigned version (only part of which is shown here) has not proved totally satisfactory. Despite improvements in the presentation it has been found that such text – unsupported by adequate illustrations – can cause difficulties, particularly with overseas operators from the Third World. A further version of this manual has now been prepared which uses illustrations and text in a step-by-step cartoon-strip procedure. The use of visuals in procedural instruction is discussed in Chapter 9.

Figure 7/6b

---

1   ■ Introduction

1.1   The balance is a sensitive piece of precision laboratory equipment,
           designed to give accurate readings over long periods of time.

1.2   Because some components may become damaged, the balances are not
           transported in an operational condition; therefore some setting-up is
           necessary after delivery.

1.3   The procedure is fully described in these instructions, but should only be
           carried out with the help of a competent mechanic or technician.

1.4   All balances are clearly marked as follows:

           export packed;
           home packed.

           ● It is clearly indicated in the text that some of the setting-up operations
           do not apply to 'home packed' balances, because they have already been
           carried out by ELE.

1.5   ● Do not attempt to carry out any other adjustment or setting other than
           those listed.

1.6   In case of difficulty, contact your supplier, agent, or ELE Service
           Department, who will be pleased to advise and assist.

2   ■ Setting-up

2.1   Place the balance on a level surface and adjust the feet (1) for non-rocking.
           It is not necessary for the balance to be precisely horizontal.

2.2   Remove weight pan cover and scoop (2 and 3).

2.3   Remove any packing underneath the weight pan support (4) and scoop
           support (5).

Chapter 8

Alternatives to prose

Three alternatives to conventional prose are described in this chapter: algorithms, information mapping, and programmed and computer-assisted instruction.

Many learners find prose text – the principal means of instructional communication – a barrier, particularly when they are not verbally inclined. Learners from different cultures also often lack the necessary verbal and intellectual skills required to understand textbooks which have been written for learners of their own age in another language.

One way to help such readers might be to consider using alternatives to prose. In this chapter we shall consider three of these:
- algorithms
- information mapping, and
- programmed and computer-assisted instruction.

Algorithms

A number of researchers have concluded that continuous prose is probably not the best vehicle for expressing complex interrelated rules, and they have turned to alternative modes of expression, particularly the *algorithm*. An algorithm may be defined as an exact prescription or recipe leading to the achievement of a specific outcome.

Algorithms may come in many forms but the two most common in instructional situations are (i) those that present material in a diagrammatic way to depict decision processes (see Figure 8/1), and (ii) those that present material in a question and answer format (see Figure 8/2). Algorithms thus provide ways of expressing complex rules, regulations, instructions and procedures in a simpler way than prose.

Thought needs to be given to whether an algorithm is always the best solution for dealing with complex problems. Some algorithms can become very complicated and in such situations other layouts may prove more suitable. Wright and Reid (1973) suggested that different formats suited different aims. In their experiment they compared the four conditions shown in Figure 8/2. They found that the prose format was the most difficult to understand and that the algorithm was best for solving difficult problems. However, they also found that the table was best for solving simple problems and that the linked statements were easier to remember. In other words, the best layout depends upon the objectives of the learner.

Although research shows that algorithms can be easier (for adults) to comprehend than their conventional prose counterparts, many adults are put off by their unconventional appearance, and many children might find them unusual – and therefore difficult. Algorithms in electronic form, however, might be very useful in helping people through lengthy procedural documents as only one question at a time need appear. Furthermore, teaching learners to write simple algorithmic statements or to construct their own contingency tables concerning a particular topic would no doubt aid their learning considerably.

Although the research suggests advantages for algorithms over complex prose, we need to note here that there is little research on the design of algorithms themselves. A recent study by Krohn (1983) suggests that performance is best when the directional orientation of the flow chart matches normal reading patterns – that is, from left to right and top to

Figure 8/1

An algorithm to show a series of
procedures and their outcomes.
Figure from Neurath, M. (1965)
Living with One Another.
London: Max Parrish. Reproduced
with permission of the author.

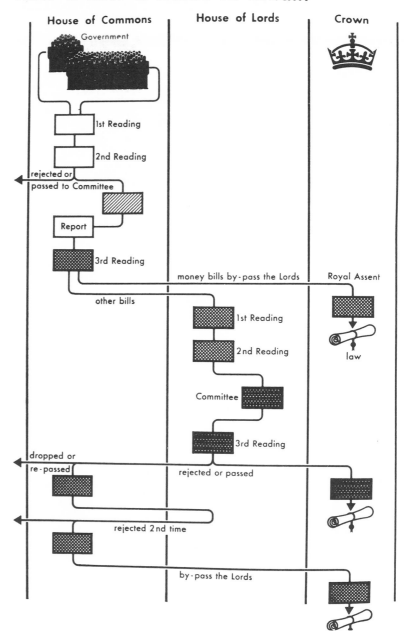

bottom. The text by Motil (1984) includes a valuable discussion of
algorithms, flow charts, block diagrams etc. It also uses an interesting
presentation technique in that each algorithm given on a left-hand page is
accompanied by a prose exposition on the right.

However, the available published guidelines on the writing of algorithms do
not appear to be based on much research evidence. Again it would seem
important to advise anyone contemplating including an algorithm in their text
that it be evaluated first with potential readers. One cannot assume that
because an algorithm has been constructed comprehension is assured.

Figure 8/2

The materials used in the experiments by Wright and Reid (1973). Reproduced with permission of the authors and the American Psychological Association. Copyright © American Psychological Association, 1973.

When time is limited, travel by Rocket, unless cost is also limited, in which case go by Space Ship. When only cost is limited an Astrobus should be used for journeys of less than 10 orbs, and a Satellite for longer journeys. Cosmocars are recommended when there are no constraints on time or cost, unless the distance to be travelled exceeds 10 orbs. For journeys longer than 10 orbs, when time and cost are not important, journeys should be made by Super Star.

Where only time is limited
travel by Rocket.

Where only cost is limited
travel by satellite if journey more than 10 orbs,
travel by astrobus if journey less than 10 orbs.

Both time and cost are limited
travel by Space Ship.

Where time and cost are not limited
travel by Super Star if journey more than 10 orbs,
travel by Cosmocar if journey less than 10 orbs.

	Journey less than 10 orbs	Journey more than 10 orbs
Where time only is limited	Travel by Rocket	Travel by Rocket
Where only cost is limited	Travel by Astrobus	Travel by Satellite
Where time and cost are not limited	Travel by Cosmocar	Travel by Super Star
Where both time and cost are limited	Travel by Space Ship	Travel by Space Ship

Is time limited?.......
.   .
yes   no
.   .
Is cost limited?   Is cost limited?.......
.   .   .   .
.   .   yes   no
.   .   .   .
.   .   Is travelling   Is travelling
.   .   distance more   distance more
.   .   than 10 orbs?   than 10 orbs?
.   .   .   .   .   .
yes   no   yes   no   yes   no
.   .   .   .   .   .
Travel by   Travel by   Travel by   Travel by   Travel by   Travel by
Space   Rocket   Satelite   Astrobus   Super   Cosmocar
Ship   Star

Structured writing and information mapping

The readers of this text must all be aware of the likely impact of the 'information explosion' on the printed word. One expert, for example, has suggested that a professional research worker might be expected to read over 60 technical documents per day to keep up with his field; another has pointed out that aircraft maintenance documents now weigh more than the planes they are supposed to maintain; a third has indicated that the number of patents published by *Chemical Abstracts* has increased from less than 200,000 during 1907-16 to between four and five million during 1967-78.

Estimates such as these suggest that in the field of technical documentation (and elsewhere) we need:
- to use computer-based storage and retrieval systems;
- to facilitate retrieval from stored information, whether computer-based or not; and
- to change our writing and our reading habits in certain areas.

Structured writing suggests one way of attempting to do all of these things.

Structured writing is the name given to a set of procedures developed by Robert Horn and his associates from the mid-1960s. These procedures help writers to organize and to display their text in the form of information maps both for learning and for reference purposes. Figure 8/3 provides an example of a one-page map which in itself explains the basic features.

This map gives the flavour and the appearance of what Horn is trying to achieve. The emphasis is on formats which communicate quickly and which facilitate scanning and retrieval. Limitations of space unfortunately forbid further illustrations. Horn's (1976) book *How to Write Information Mapping* contains over 400 pages, and a recent paper (Horn, 1985) has over 50 maps. These fuller accounts are essential reading for interested readers.

Anyone who inspects Horn's 'before and after' examples will see immediately that information retrieval is highly facilitated when one pays more attention to the layout and the presentation of the text. This is indeed the argument of this present book. Horn and I might disagree over the details, but we are together on this point. It seems to me that structured writing is best suited for text that can be presented in standard formats (eg research summaries), and less suitable for non-standard presentations (such as the chapters in this book). Personally, I find non-standard text set in information maps difficult to read (but easier to review).

Programmed and computer-assisted instruction

A rather different approach to text design can be seen in the exemplars of programmed instruction. Here the emphasis is on teaching and learning rather than on following procedures or on rapid retrieval. Programmed materials may be presented in a textbook or in an electronic format, but whatever method is used the basic principles are as follows:

1. The learner reads the text and works with it individually, at his or her own rate.

2. The learner works through a carefully ordered sequence of items (called frames), which are usually short, and each frame leads directly on to the next.

Figure 8/3

An illustration of information
mapping (courtesy of Robert Horn).

VISIBLE AND INVISIBLE FEATURES OF INFORMATION MAP BOOKS

Introduction	Information maps for self-instructional books are conspicuous for their physical features, the format in which they present information. An equally important aspect of such information maps, however, is that the content itself is selected and organized according to a set of underlying principles. The method of presentation and the organization of content, may be thought of as the visible and invisible features of a mapped page.
Visible Features	The more obvious visible characteristics are these: • information is presented in blocks • marginal labels identify the kind of information in each block • a consistent format is used for each kind of information : procedures follow one format, concept maps follow another distinct format, and so on • functional and uniform headings and subheadings are used to make scanning easy and to speed up reference work • each information map begins on a new page, and, in programs for initial learning, most maps occupy single pages • feedback questions and answers are located in close proximity to the relevant information maps • a local index at the bottom of maps provides page numbers for quick location of prerequisite topics (The last two features are not used in technical reports.)
Invisible Features	The arrangement and sequencing of materials presented in information map formats are the result of: • detailed specification of learning and reference objectives in behavioural terms • specification of prerequisites for the subject-matter area • classification of the subject matter into component types (concepts, procedures, etc.) • definition of the contingencies required for successful learning and reference

3. Each frame normally asks the learner to respond to it in some way, eg by writing an answer down, or by choosing a particular answer and consequent page to turn to (in text) or consequent key to press (on a microcomputer).

4. The learner is usually informed immediately after making the response whether or not it is correct. This is often simply done by displaying the correct answer.

5. The material is so written that the learner normally makes few errors.

In the early days of programmed learning it was conventional to distinguish between *linear* programs of the kind described above and *branching* programs where each frame that the students were directed to depended on their response to the preceding one. With computer-assisted instruction (CAI) it is possible to provide more elaborate branching routines (based, for example, on the students' prior knowledge, or their speed of responding) but this occurs more in theory than in practice.

Initially there was much discussion concerning the relative merits of linear versus branching sequences, writing versus choosing responses, using large instructional steps instead of small ones, and so on. Compromise solutions appeared. These early debates subsided to be replaced later with questions such as: Does a learner *have* to make a response to *every* frame? Is it always necessary to give correct answers? When is it appropriate to ask a multiple-choice question? When might a careful linear exposition in short steps be most appropriate? Can this particular point be made best with an illustration? Is it more appropriate to use lengthy prose passages – with occasional questions – at certain times? How might one integrate workbooks or films with the text? And so on. Modern programs are thus much more flexible than the traditional ones which are well known.

Design considerations

Although there is evidence that programmed materials work, there is, unfortunately, no clear evidence as to *why* they actually do so. Writing programs is a pragmatic procedure. Despite the fact that there are several guidelines, there are no clear rules about how to write frames, nor about how to design the layout of programmed materials.

Experience with CAI suggests that the design of each frame can dramatically affect the sequence in which it is scanned by students. Steinberg (1984) includes a list of rules of thumb with respect to designing frames on CAI: it is important that frames are uncluttered and layouts consistent; it is better to let the learner control the rate of display; and scrolling (see Chapter 13) should be avoided. Steinberg also considers the advantages of animation, but points out that poorly designed graphics may interfere with learning.

Programmed materials presented in electronic form face particular difficulties because many are presented on a small screen: a typical text grid of 80 characters by 24 lines drastically reduces the amount of information that can be presented on each frame. Conventional programmed textbooks have more flexibility in the amount they can present per page (particularly if A4 is used) and thus they are better able to use space to convey the structure of the text to the learner. Electronic texts, however, have the advantages of less bulky storage, more flexibility in terms of branching, and more possibilities in terms of colour. All of these issues are discussed further in Chapter 13.

The design of a text, of course, can have quite a marked effect upon its appearance. Figure 8/4a on the next page shows the original layout of a linear programmed text. Figure 8/4b shows a revised version based upon a suggestion by Paul Luna.

There has been very little research comparing the effects of such design decisions within one particular format (such as linear or branching). One study (Biran, 1967) did compare two formats of a branching program: a 'scrambled text' version, where the learner had to turn to different pages in order to work through the program, and a simpler layout where the answers to the various choices were presented sequentially. In the simpler version each left-hand page contained a 'main sequence' item, complete with its multiple-choice question, and each corresponding right-hand page contained a confirmation of the correct choice and 'remedial' items corresponding to each of the wrong choices. The sequential version took almost twice as much paper as the original scrambled version (60:33 pages). However, in this study the sequential version produced the higher test scores, required less study time and elicited fewer critical comments from the learners.

Although research on design features within a specific format has been limited there has been some research comparing more global formats. Several studies comparing branching programs with linear ones have suggested that branching programs can teach as effectively as, and often more quickly than, linear ones, especially with adults. Work with young children, however, has suggested that linear programs often do better than branching ones (although they usually take longer).

More recently a number of investigators have started to compare programmed texts with materials designed using information mapping techniques. Horn (1985) summarized two such studies, both of which showed advantages for the mapping technique.

Summary

1. **Algorithms provide exact prescriptions leading to specific outcomes. Although effective in particular instances, there has been little research on their design.**

2. **Structured writing is a method for organizing categories of information and displaying it – both for learning and for reference purposes. The emphasis is on formats which communicate quickly and which facilitate scanning and retrieval.**

3. **Programmed materials are concerned with teaching and learning. A distinction can be drawn between programmed instruction (what the writer does in preparing programmed materials) and programmed learning (what the learner does when studying a program). Combining these procedures leads to effective instruction.**

4. **Differences in the design of programmed texts can produce differences in their appearance for the learner, and such differences can be evaluated. CAI has additional design constraints which can present additional problems.**

Figure 8/4a

An extract from *Programmed Instruction: What It Is and How It Works* by Ohmer Milton and Leonard J. West. Copyright © Harcourt Brace Jovanovich Inc, 1961, and reproduced with their permission.

	A second important condition for efficient learning is the presentation of subject matter in a series of <u>small</u> <u>logical</u> steps. The learner must master Step A before he can grasp _____ B. 20
Step 20	An ancient Greek fable tells us that Milo was able to lift his full-grown bull because he had lifted it daily since it was a calf. Since the animal had <u>small</u> increases in weight daily, Milo's weight-lifting "program" progressed through a series of many_____ steps. 21
small 21	Unfortunately, under usual classroom conditions it is difficult for the instructor to present subject matter in steps which are sufficiently _____ in size. 22
small 22	A later item in this program - to which you probably cannot yet respond correctly - reads: "Another condition is that each response is followed by . . .". That item is a large step beyond the present one. However, after being led through many _____ steps, you will later be able to _____ correctly. 23
small respond 23	This program may seem annoyingly simple, but the merit of a step-by-step presentation of subject matter is shown by the fact that you have made few, if any, incorrect_____ to the statements or stimuli of this program. 24
responses 24	

Figure 8/4b

A redesigned layout for Figure 8/4a.

20

A second important condition for efficient learning is the presentation of the subject matter in a series of <u>small</u> <u>logical</u> steps.
The learner must master Step A before he can grasp _____ B.

Step

21

An ancient Greek fable tells us that Milo was able to lift his full-grown bull because he had lifted it daily since it was a calf.
Since the animal had <u>small</u> increases in weight daily, Milo's weight-lifting 'program' progressed through a series of many _____ steps.

small

22

Unfortunately, under usual classroom conditions it is difficult for the instructor to present subject matter in steps which are sufficiently _____ in size.

small

23

A later item in this program - to which you probably cannot yet respond correctly - reads: "Another condition is that each response is followed by . . .". That item is a large step beyond the present one.
However, after being led through many _____ steps, you will later be able to _____ correctly.

small
respond

24

This program may seem annoyingly simple, but the merit of a step-by-step presentation of subject matter is shown by the fact that you have made few, if any, incorrect _____ to the statements or stimuli of this program.

responses

Chapter 9

The role of illustrations

In this chapter research on the function and effectiveness of illustrations is briefly outlined. Attention is drawn to the importance of the positioning and labelling of illustrations, to the use of pictures in teaching procedural routines, and to the problems of using additional colour in illustrations.

In this text I have been involved so far in the discussion of signs. Words, spaces, and illustrations are all signs, but they are signs of different sorts. (Strictly speaking they are all sign-vehicles or sign-carriers, since the signs, or meanings, come from the reader.)

It is conventional to classify signs as being either iconic or digital. An *iconic* sign is one which in some way resembles the thing it stands for. Photographs, drawings and illustrations in general are iconic because they resemble in some way their referents. A *digital* sign need not resemble its referent in any way. Words, numbers, semaphore signs, and the Morse code are all examples of digital signs. To interpret and understand the sign, the receiver must know the code. Sometimes, of course, iconic and digital sign systems are combined – as in text with illustrations, illustrations with captions, and symbols which use explanatory labels (see Figure 9/1). In the isotype system of picture communication (see Chapter 10), a symbol is iconic but it becomes a member of a digital system when it is combined systematically with others to make a statement about something.

Figure 9/1

Traffic signs provide examples of iconic and digital signs, and also combinations of the two.

(1) Road works: iconic.

(2) Ford: digital.

(3) Axle weight limit: iconic and digital.

(1)   (2)   (3)

Textbook authors and designers need to be aware of the various functions that are best fulfilled by different sorts of sign. Twyman (1979) has put forward a comprehensive classification scheme for this purpose. Here a summary of research findings in this area follows, although this summary, of course, provides only generalities which may not apply in every specific case, and for all types of reader.

Illustrations in text

Illustrations are interesting in their own right – thus they may *attract* or *distract* the reader. Words, on the other hand, are not particularly interesting as things in themselves – it is the ideas conveyed by the words that matter. Because illustrations are interesting they may lead to the reading of the text, and so their positioning is very important. I shall return to this point later.

Illustrations are good for conveying concrete images (eg a picture of an elephant may be 'worth a thousand words'), and thus they are good for providing support material when teaching a concept. Words on the other hand are good for conveying abstract ideas and for communicating concepts *which have already been learned*. (For example, the word 'mammal' is probably worth several pictures.) Words can convey propositional concepts such as 'would be', 'might be', and 'should be' better than illustrations. If the information can be readily conveyed in words, then there may be no need for a picture. Conversely, illustrations are a good way of avoiding technical jargon. Figure 9/2 is a more effective way of communicating the instruction 'see that the sliding dog associated with the reverse drive bevel is rotating freely before tightening the long differential casing'.

Figure 9/2

(Reproduced with permission of Patricia Wright.)

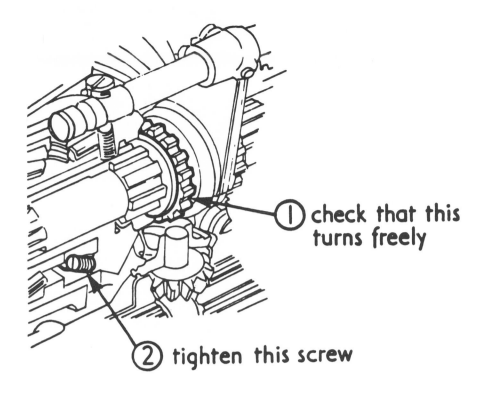

Illustrations are useful for conveying visual concepts (eg what Margaret Thatcher looks like) and spatial concepts (eg the relative size of objects), although, in some cultures, two-dimensional representations of three-dimensional objects cause some difficulty. Temporal concepts can be translated into visual ones (clock faces, musical notation, time-charts, etc), but translations of time into space involve conventions which must be learned. Authors must either teach the code or be sure their readers know it.

Illustrations and diagrams are good for conveying ideas that have to be considered simultaneously – they allow learners to make multiple discriminations easily. Words, on the other hand, are possibly better for conveying ideas that have to be treated sequentially: thus words *may* be more important when the order in which the ideas are encountered is critical (eg in reading a poem or in following a set of instructions). The use of cartoon strips for instruction, however, shows just how valuable is the joint production of printed words and pictures.

One approach to assessing the effectiveness of illustrations has been to consider them in terms of what readers use them for. Some authors have suggested, for instance, that illustrations may fulfil one or more of the following roles in instructional text:

1. An affective role — enhancing interest and motivation
2. An attentional role — attracting and directing attention
3. A didactic role — facilitating learning by showing rather than telling and by providing additional information
4. A supportive role — enhancing the learning of less able readers
5. A retentional role — facilitating long-term recall.

Recent studies have examined all of these roles, but most have attempted to examine the didactic role of illustrations: it is to these studies that I shall now turn.

Clearly in such studies there are a large number of variables to consider, and at first sight it seems difficult to formulate a general picture. Researchers have worked with different kinds of text (from children's readers to technical manuals), used different kinds of illustration (from line drawings to coloured photographs), studied different groups of readers (from young to old, with high and low ability) and measured different aims with different kinds of measuring technique (from factual recall to drawing).

One recently developed statistical technique called meta-analysis, however, allows researchers to pool together all the studies on one particular topic and to look for average overall effects. Levie and Lentz (1982) used this approach with over 40 studies to consider the didactic role played by illustrations. Levie and Lentz first found that they had to distinguish in these studies between three sources of information in illustrated text. These were:
1. information provided only in the illustration(s);
2. information available in both the illustrations and the text; and
3. information provided only in the text.

They then asked (from the pooled studies) whether or not the illustrations aided the recall of information from all three sources. The results were surprisingly clear. They found (overall) that there were marked effects for the recall of *text that was illustrated*. They wrote:

'In 46 experimental comparisons of reading with and without pictures, the presence of relevant illustrations helped the learning of illustrated text information in all but one case. In 85 per cent of the cases, the improvement was statistically significant. On the average, groups reading with pictures learned one-third more, an improvement equal to one-half a standard deviation of groups reading without pictures.'

Levie and Lentz also found (overall) that the presence of illustrations had a hardly measurable effect on the recall of information that was *not* illustrated. They wrote:

'In 20 experimental comparisons, groups reading with pictures learned slightly more non-illustrated text information in 11 cases and slightly less than or the same as groups reading without pictures in 9 cases. Overall, groups reading with pictures scored just 5 per cent better on tests of learning non-illustrated information. Hence, the positive learning effects of illustrations are specific to the information provided by them.'

Thus, it appears that pictures have an additive function in instructional text: they aid the recall of the material that they illustrate, and they do this without really helping the recall of other non-illustrated text.

Levie and Lentz make particular mention of the work of Francis Dwyer in their article. Dwyer has carried out over 100 studies in this field and his work is important because:
1. he has varied the types of illustration he has used;
2. he has varied the kinds of test he has used to measure their effectiveness; and
3. he has varied the media and conditions that he used in his experiments.

Dwyer experimented with a 2,000-word passage on the human heart and eight types of illustration. These eight types were chosen to represent a continuum of realism as follows:
• Simple line drawings (black and white)
• Simple line drawings (coloured)
• Detailed and shaded drawings (black and white)
• Detailed and shaded drawings (coloured)

- Photographs of a model (black and white)
- Photographs of a model (coloured)
- Realistic photographs (black and white)
- Realistic photographs (coloured)

The tests Dwyer used were:
- A *drawing* test: participants were provided with a list of specific terms and asked to draw and label a diagram of the heart appropriately.
- A 20-item multiple-choice *identification* test: participants were asked to identify numbered items on a drawing of the heart.
- A 20-item multiple-choice *terminology* test: participants were required to demonstrate knowledge of specific terms and concepts.
- A 20-item multiple-choice *comprehension* test: participants were required to demonstrate a thorough understanding of the heart, its parts and its internal functioning.
- An *overall* test score was arrived at, based on scores obtained on all the tests listed above.

Experiments using these materials and tests were conducted with various media – eg prose text, workbooks, programmed instruction, tape-slides, film, television, etc – and with learners who varied in age, ability, motivation, and prior knowledge, to list just some of the variables.

Dwyer's main findings were many and various, but the major findings were as follows:
1. There was no relationship between the test scores and the realism of the illustrations.
2. Different results were found on different tests: thus participants with illustrations did best on the drawing test, next best on the identification test, next the terminology test, and worst on the comprehension test. On this latter test they did not perform better than participants in control groups without illustrations.
3. Different results were found with different media. Simple line drawings, for instance, were more effective with paced media (slides, television) whereas more detailed illustrations were more effective in self-paced media (text, programmed instruction).
4. Colour did not prove to be an effective device for all the tests and media: in the text presentations, however, colour did prove useful.

Dwyer presented many more findings than these and more detailed accounts can be found (Dwyer, 1972; 1976; 1978). The findings are, of course, restricted to the narrow range of materials used and the quality of their presentation. Holliday (1973) presents an interesting critical discussion of some of Dwyer's earlier findings in the context of science education.

Positioning and labelling illustrations

There has been little satisfactory research on the positioning of illustrations in relation to the text. Illustrations are frequently put at the top or the bottom of a page without reference to where they are mentioned in the text. Often, because of their size, they may be positioned on a following page. A study by Bogusch (1983) showed, however, that when illustrations were positioned close to their textual references, then placement to the left, right, above, below or even randomly in the text had no effect on the performance or preferences of her ten-year-old participants.

Clearly it is not always easy to position illustrations directly after their first textual reference – especially if the illustrations are large and frequent and the text is minimal (as I have found in preparing this text). None the less, one might imagine that readers would prefer illustrations to appear immediately after the first textual reference than to have them positioned inconsistently in this respect. It is for reasons such as these that I have on occasions in this text completed subsections in chapters with their illustrations and then started a new subsection with its illustrations on a following page.

The positioning of illustrations is important because of their attentional role: if illustrations are divorced from the text then readers are less likely to look at them or to look at them for less time. One way to focus attention on illustrations is to refer to them directly in the text (using such phrases as 'See Figure 1'). Another is to label different parts of the illustration. A third way is to use captions. Brody (1982) reports that Gombrich deemed captions to be one of the most critical variables in the understanding of pictures.

Labels and captions need to be presented in a consistent manner throughout the text, and their positioning is important too. Centred captions, for instance, vary their starting point from the left-hand margin according to the length of the caption. Simple captions (eg 'Figure 10') thus 'get lost' if they are centred and if all the other captions are lengthy.

Pictures and procedural instructions

Step-by-step pictures and their captions are a common enough instructional device, but there has been little research on their design or their effectiveness. Figure 9/3 provides a typical example where the spatial layout represents a temporal sequence. The instructions shown in Figure 9/3 seem clear but perhaps they might be better if the captions were placed appropriately beneath each picture. Furthermore, it might be helpful to repeat before each task the general instructions given in the Preface of this instruction manual – as readers will hardly refer to the Preface each time they use the text. These instructions, incidentally, are:
- Read the appropriate section carefully, right through before you start.
- Take careful note of any warning in the text.
- When doing a job read the individual stage caption in relation to the illustration to which it refers. Do not simply follow the pictures or skim the text.

The limited research that there is on the use of pictures and diagrams to aid procedural tasks is somewhat confusing but it does suggest the value of illustrations. A study by Booher (1975), for instance, compared the following types of instruction for three procedural tasks:
1. text only
2. pictures only
3. mainly text (but with related pictures)
4. mainly pictures (but with related text)
5. text (with redundant pictures)
6. pictures (with redundant text)

Booher found that for all three tasks Condition 4 (mainly pictures but with related text) and Condition 6 (pictures with redundant text) were the most successful. Similar findings were reported in a recent study by Jonathan Hawley – one of my undergraduate students. Hawley found in a knot-tying

Figure 9/3

An example of a visual aid to a procedural task. (Figure reproduced with permission from *Mending Things in Pictures*, Wolfe Publishing Ltd, 1976.)

replace ceramic wall tile

1   A tile which has been badly broken can be picked out piece by piece to leave a neat square to be filled.

2   A really hard blow may have damaged the plaster underneath. This must be repaired with filler.

3   Tile adhesive is applied using a spreader comb and the tile pushed into place level with surrounding tiles.

4   After a day, the gaps can be filled with tile grout. When this is dry, polish with a newspaper.

5   Do not try to remove a tile in one piece because you will probably break adjacent ones. Break it!

6   A tip when mounting accessories on a wall and tiles need to be drilled. A strip of sticky tape will stop the masonry drill tip from wandering.

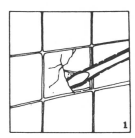
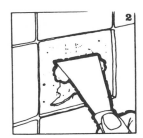

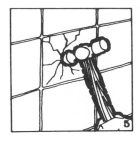

task that a sequence of photographs with instructions on the reverse was more effective than the same sequence with instructions printed directly above the photographs. Hawley attributed this to the fact that the participants with the photographs with instructions on the reverse were not distracted by the instructions, and only referred to them if they wished.

One problem here (which is common to all studies with pictures) is that there are good and bad pictures: how far does the quality of what is actually shown in a picture affect learning? Relatively little research has been done on this problem, but work by Szlichcinski (1984) has shown that alternative drawings of the same procedure can produce different effects.

Finally in this section I shall comment briefly on the use of comic strips or cartoons in instruction. Clearly the affective role of instructions is to the fore in comic strips: their aim being to attract and motivate less able learners (see

Figure 9/4). Often strip cartoons are used to present a simplified form of instruction, but there has been little research on their effectiveness in this respect. Some variations that offer themselves for research seem to be:
- upper- versus lower-case dialogue
- balloon speech versus boxed speech
- the amount of text per balloon
- the size of the print
- the integration of cartoons with conventional text, etc.

The general picture that emerges from studies of text with cartoon embellishments is that cartoons often enhance motivation, but they do not often increase comprehension.

Figure 9/4

Comic-strip cartoon presentations can be an effective way of communication — but care still needs to be taken over their design. (Figure reproduced from the pamphlet *Good Health* with permission of the Health Education Council.)

Learning to read text and illustrations

It is well known that learning to read text is a complex skill that is painstakingly acquired. It is perhaps not so obvious but the same thing applies in learning to read illustrations and other tabular and graphic materials. Learning to read text may be aided by illustrations, and learning to read illustrations may be aided by text.

Studies of the effects of illustrations in helping children learn to read at first sight seem to produce contradictory findings. These contradictions are resolved, however, when the studies are divided into two kinds. It seems that pictures can *hinder* comprehension when children are learning the meaning of individual vocabulary items one at a time. However, pictures can *help* comprehension when children are learning to read meaningful text and if, as indicated in the previous section, the pictures supplement the information given in the text.

In point of fact very little seems to be known about how children learn to interpret pictures and how they develop skills in this respect. Some researchers, for instance, have suggested that it is not until the ages of six to eight that children can reliably compare two pictures or diagrams and judge whether they are identical in all respects. Other workers have suggested that this occurs a little earlier – depending upon the type of task the child is asked to do (see Murphy and Wood, 1981). Several studies have shown that children find pictures ambiguous, that they are unable to interpret depth cues in pictures, that they have difficulty in interpreting action elements, and that changes in scale are confusing. Similar findings have also been reported in studies of how adults who are unable to read interpret pictures.

Authors of textbooks, therefore, need to assess the value of their illustrations. This can be done, somewhat crudely, by asking potential readers to comment on, explain, or discuss the proposed illustrative material with the author present. Another possibility might be that texts could be produced with occasional blank pages so that illustrations appropriate to the reader's own culture might be drawn in by the teachers or the readers themselves. Some recent research shows that allowing children to illustrate their own materials leads to superior learning, although it is not clear that this would work with very young children. Guidelines for authors concerning illustrations in overseas textbooks are available (see Zimmerman and Perkin, 1982), and these might be studied profitably by authors of books for young children.

What are the functions of colour?

Colour – like illustrations – is used in the printing of instructional materials for two rather different purposes. Colour can be used functionally to aid the instruction, or for aesthetic and motivational reasons.

Most people seem to agree that coloured illustrations are desirable from a *motivational* point of view, although the research suggests that the motivational effect of pictorial illustrations varies greatly with the age, the intelligence and the education of the reader. Younger and less intelligent children pay more attention to illustrations than do older more intelligent ones.

Some researchers, however, have gone as far as to suggest that the prime function of most coloured illustrations in textbooks is to make the product more marketable, and that much of the pictorial material to which children are exposed (particularly in young children's early reading books) is designed more in terms of adult tastes than in terms of the learning requirements of children.

A prime example of the functional use of colour is that provided by the map of the London Underground system. Here several different colours are used, each to denote a separate route. It is often suggested that such a functional use of colour is a useful ingredient in line drawings and illustrations (particularly of the technical, medical and biological kind). Indeed, Dwyer's research discussed earlier showed this to be true. In his 1978 text, Dwyer reviewed his studies on the effectiveness of colour in illustrations and listed over 30 studies (in addition to his own) that showed colour to be an effective instructional variable.

None the less, in view of the earlier discussion on learning to read illustrations, it might be expected that the conventions we adults accept so naturally concerning the use of colour in illustrations would have to be taught to children. In many situations the use of full colour is essential if learners are to make correct discriminations. The debate about whether or not to use colour, and if so how much colour to use, arises in situations when colour is not absolutely necessary. Particular difficulties can then arise with (i) using too many colours indiscriminately, and (ii) using too few colours (say only two) to denote more than two functions.

In a useful review of the functions of a second colour, Waller *et al* (1982) point out that a second colour may be useful:
- where pointed lines linking labels to diagrams might be confusing if only one colour is used;
- where a coloured grid might be superimposed over a black and white illustration to indicate, for example, some sort of grouping; and
- where there might be two or more levels of text running in parallel (eg study guidance being differentiated by colour from mainstream subject matter).

I would argue here that if only one or two extra colours are being used, then they must be used consistently and only when it seems necessary to make a point. There is no need to use colour on every page simply because it is technically possible to do so.

In specifying the use of colour printing it is useful to keep the following points in mind:
1. About 8.5 per cent of males and 0.5 per cent of females are colour blind to some extent.
2. If reference is to be made by the author or the teacher to the function of the colour, then the colour must have a name in the language of the reader.
3. A pale colour, visible when seen as a large area, may be almost invisible when used to print a word or a fine line.
4. A dark colour will appear almost black when used to print a word or a fine line.
5. Bright colours set up a dazzle effect when printed as words or fine lines.

6. Black ink printed on white paper has the best contrast value.
7. Legibility is impaired when black text is printed on a coloured ground.
8. Legibility is severely impaired when text is printed over a broken ground such as an illustration or a photograph.
9. Strong colour or a strong pattern in black and white or colour will be an irritant if it is positioned close to the text at the periphery of the visual field.
10. If the printed page is liable to be copied using photographic or other means, then the coloured parts will appear as black or grey, or may disappear completely.

For all these reasons the designer will have to consider whether the use of colour is worthwhile.

Summary

1. **It is possible to distinguish between *iconic* signs (symbols which resemble the things they stand for) and *digital* signs (symbols which need not resemble their referents).**

2. **Illustrations serve a variety of overlapping functions in instructions: they can aid motivation, attention, instruction and retention.**

3. **The research suggests that illustrations aid the recall of text that is illustrated, but that they do not help the recall of related (but not illustrated) text.**

4. **The positioning and the labelling of illustrations is important for drawing the reader's attention to particular points in the text.**

5. **The design aspects of strip cartoons for instructional purposes have not been adequately researched.**

6. **Children have to learn the conventions used in illustrations that adults take for granted.**

7. **Additional colour in printing is often unnecessary and can cause additional problems.**

Chapter 10

Tables and graphs

Chapters 10 and 11 present guidelines for displaying quantitative information. Tables and graphs require as much care in their design and positioning as does the text itself.

Chapters 10 and 11 consider some – but by no means all – of the ways of displaying quantitative information. The topics considered in this chapter are tables and graphs.

Tables

Tables vary enormously in their complexity and detail. As Patricia Wright (1980) remarks, 'One of the striking similarities between prose and tables is the diversity of the materials to be found under each umbrella term. While prose varies from romantic short stories to lengthy physics textbooks, so tables vary from those which are entirely numerical (eg logarithmic tables) to those which are entirely verbal or use other symbolic notation (eg the periodic table of chemical elements)'.

According to Wright three processes determine how easy it is for readers to use a table. These are:
1. *Comprehension processes* – do readers understand how the table has been organized?
2. *Search processes* – do readers know where to look to find the answers to their questions?
3. *Interpretative processes* – do readers know how to interpret the answers that they find in the table? Do the answers provide all they need to know or do they need to compare these figures with other figures in this, or other tables?

The more complex the table, the more difficult is each of these three processes. Children in particular have trouble with complex tables and it is clear that we all have to acquire the conventions of reading and using graphic materials. In what ways might designers make our task more simple?

Simplifying the content

Ehrenberg (1977) argues that most statistical tables are badly presented and that their understanding requires a great deal of effort – even from sophisticated users. The criterion for a good table, according to Ehrenberg, is that patterns and exceptions should be obvious at a glance – at least once one knows what they are.

Ehrenberg provides four basic rules for presenting data in tables:

1. Drastically round off numbers so that readers can easily make meaningful comparisons. (Compare Table 10/1 with Table 10/2.)

2. Include averages. Averages not only summarize the data but they also allow one to grasp the spread between the above-average and the below-average values. (Compare Table 10/2 with Table 10/3.)

3. Figures in columns are easier to compare than figures in rows. (Compare Table 10/3 with Table 10/4.)

4. Order rows in columns by size. Larger numbers placed at the top help mental arithmetic. Ordering by size aids comparison. (This rule is more appropriate for single tables than for a series of tables where the order of sizes may vary; for a series of tables one must keep to the same order.)

Table 10/1

Thousands unemployed	1966	1968	1970	1973
Total	330.9	549.5	582.2	597.9
Males	259.6	460.7	495.3	499.4
Females	71.3	88.8	86.9	98.5

Table 10/2

Thousands unemployed	1966	1968	1970	1973
Total	330	550	580	600
Males	260	460	500	500
Females	71	89	87	99

Table 10/3

Thousands unemployed	1966	1968	1970	1973	Average
Total	330	550	580	600	520
Males	260	460	500	500	430
Females	71	89	87	99	86

Table 10/4

	Unemployed (1000s)		
	Males	Females	Total
1973	500	99	600
1970	500	87	580
1968	460	89	550
1966	260	71	330
Average	430	86	520

Readers are referred to Ehrenberg's (1977) article for a fuller discussion of these guidelines.

Spacing the items

Simple tables, of the sort shown in Ehrenberg's examples, may suffer in clarity if they are presented in justified form and if, in particular, they are spread or squeezed to match the width of the text. This can be particularly unfortunate if there are, say, only two columns in the table. My own research has shown that simple tables ranged from the left-hand margin can be read just as easily as balanced or centred tables, and that left-ranging tables are considerably easier to type. Table 10/5 below shows the traditional approach to table design. Table 10/6 shows the approach I would suggest. In Table 10/6 the eye movements between the columns in the table are small and regular unlike those in Table 10/5.

Table 10/5
Distribution of places of meeting of spouses.

Place of meeting	%
Dance or dance hall	27.3
Private house	17.6
Work or Forces	14.6
Street or public transport	9.7
Cafe or pub	6.1

Table 10/6 Distribution of places of meeting of spouses.

%	Place of meeting
27.3	Dance or dance hall
17.6	Private house
14.6	Work or Forces
9.7	Street or public transport
6.1	Cafe or pub

This argument can be taken further. If, in certain tables some elements have consistent widths and some have variable ones, then it might be easier for the reader (as well as for the printer) to put all of the consistent items together. Table 10/7 shows an original format for a set of tables in a college prospectus. Table 10/8 shows a revision to this format: now the consistent items have been placed in sequence and the text is no longer justified. This revision allowed all of the 200 or so tables in the prospectus to be spaced consistently: with the original layout each table had to be planned separately, and each looked different.

Table 10/7 Original design for a timetable in a college prospectus.

Class	Subject	Day	Times	Room
73005	Children's garments	Fri.	10-12	315
73015	Dress	Tues.	2- 4	315
73105	Embroidery	Mon.	1½- 4	315
73135	Ladies' tailoring	Fri.	2- 4	Ov15
73155	Soft furnishings	Tues.	10-12	315

Table 10/8 Revised design.

Class	Day	Time	Room	Subject
73005	Fri.	10-12	315	Children's garments
73015	Tues.	2- 4	315	Dress
73105	Mon.	1½- 4	315	Embroidery
73135	Fri.	2- 4	Ov15	Ladies' tailoring
73155	Tues.	10-12	315	Soft furnishings

Finally we might note that spacing may be used to group and separate items in tables, and thus facilitate search and retrieval. If the columns are lengthy then regular line-spacing (about every five items) aids in this respect. In addition extra headings may be useful for lengthy tables. Table 10/9 shown below, for instance, was markedly improved in its effectiveness by making the simple alterations shown in Table 10/10. Regular line-spacing was introduced between groups of items and extra side headings were provided. By changing the position of the entry 'London' people in the United Kingdom were able to compare much more easily the price of foods in other countries with those in London – the actual aim of the table.

Table 10/9

	Rumpsteak	Pork chops	Potatoes	Butter	Margarine	Cheese
Athens	0.70 - 11	0.65 + 8	0.07 + 2	0.66 + 9	0.33 - 8	0.41 + 1
Bonn	1.35 - 11	0.97 + 3	0.03	0.71 + 2	0.37 + 4	1.05 + 32
Brussels	1.21 + 1	0.82 + 11	0.02	0.58 - 3	0.26 - 9	0.54 - 9
Copenhagen	1.47 + 14	0.33 + 6	0.07 + 3	0.67 + 13	0.27 - 4	0.75 + 14
Dublin	0.75 + 20	0.82 + 15	0.06 + 2	0.47 + 10	0.33 + 9	0.53 + 13
Geneva	2.30 + 9	1.30 - 3	0.09 + 2	0.70 + 2	0.45 - 7	0.98 + 4
Hague	1.07	0.76 + 1	0.06	0.57	0.16 - 1½	0.72
London	1.34 + 33	0.72 + 3	0.04	0.31 + 7	0.29 + 5	0.42 + 2
Luxembourg	1.30 + 9	0.65 + 11	0.02	0.58 + 3	0.32 + 2	0.80
Oslo	0.94 - 68	1.12 + 7	0.07 - 1	0.42 + 2	0.21 - 8	0.59 + 14
Paris	1.32 + 25	0.83 + 15	0.04 - 2	0.71 + 9	0.29 + 1	0.55 + 25
Rome	1.21 + 10	0.85 + 8	0.04 - 1½	0.85 + 12	0.15 + 5½	0.76 + 3
Stockholm	1.28 + 6	0.91 + 2	0.08 + 1	0.56	0.35 - 15	0.74 + 4
Vienna	1.21 + 6	0.89 + 1	0.09 + 5	0.61 + 3	0.34 + 2	0.58 + 8

The plus/minus figures are changes in the past six months. Prices in £ per pound.

Table 10/10

	Rumpsteak	Pork chops	Potatoes	Butter	Margarine	Cheese	
London	1.34 + 33	0.72 + 3	0.04	0.31 + 7	0.29 + 5	0.42 + 2	London
Athens	0.70 - 11	0.65 + 8	0.07 + 2	0.66 + 9	0.33 - 8	0.41 + 1	Athens
Bonn	1.35 - 11	0.97 + 3	0.03	0.71 + 2	0.37 + 4	1.05 + 32	Bonn
Brussels	1.21 + 1	0.82 + 11	0.02	0.58 - 3	0.26 - 9	0.54 - 9	Brussels
Copenhagen	1.47 + 14	0.33 + 6	0.07 + 3	0.67 + 13	0.27 - 4	0.75 + 14	Copenhagen
Dublin	0.75 + 20	0.82 + 15	0.06 + 2	0.47 + 10	0.33 + 9	0.53 + 13	Dublin
Geneva	2.30 + 9	1.30 - 3	0.09 + 2	0.70 + 2	0.45 - 7	0.98 + 4	Geneva
Hague	1.07	0.76 + 1	0.06	0.57	0.16 - 1½	0.72	Hague
Luxembourg	1.30 + 9	0.65 + 11	0.02	0.58 + 3	0.32 + 2	0.80	Luxembourg
Oslo	0.94 - 68	1.12 + 7	0.07 - 1	0.42 + 2	0.21 - 8	0.59 + 14	Oslo
Paris	1.32 + 25	0.83 + 15	0.04 - 2	0.71 + 9	0.29 + 1	0.55 + 25	Paris
Rome	1.21 + 10	0.85 + 8	0.04 - 1½	0.85 + 12	0.15 + 5½	0.76 + 3	Rome
Stockholm	1.28 + 6	0.91 + 2	0.08 + 1	0.56	1.35 - 15	0.74 + 4	Stockholm
Vienna	1.21 + 6	0.89 + 1	0.09 + 5	0.61 + 3	0.34 + 2	0.58 + 8	Vienna

The plus/minus figures are changes in the past six months. Prices in £ per pound.

The examples given here show that tables can be designed to present information clearly without the use of printers' lines or 'rules'. The use of horizontal rules can help to group information but an excessive use of rules should be avoided. Completely boxing-in tables is not usually necessary and complicating the typesetting in this way reduces clarity. However, if rules of different thicknesses must be used to group data it is not advisable to use more than two clearly differentiated thicknesses of line.

Organizing the content

The organization of the content of tables needs to reflect the searcher's task in using the table. Often with simple materials (such as a calendar) it does not matter much if the days are listed vertically or horizontally. But, even here, if a designer takes a decorative rather than a functional approach, the result can be difficult to use. Try working out what the date will be three weeks on Saturday in Table 10/11, for example.

Table 10/11

JANUARY

FRI	SAT	SUN	MON	TUE	WED	THU	FRI	SAT	SUN	MON	TUE	WED	THU	FRI	SAT	SUN	MON	TUE	WED
1	2	3	4	5	6	7	8	9	10	11	12	13	14	15	16	17	18	19	20

THU	FRI	SAT	SUN	MON	TUE	WED	THU	FRI	SAT	SUN
21	22	23	24	25	26	27	28	29	30	31

FEBRUARY

MON	TUE	WED	THU	FRI	SAT	SUN	MON	TUE	WED	THU	FRI	SAT	SUN	MON	TUE	WED	THU	FRI	SAT
1	2	3	4	5	6	7	8	9	10	11	12	13	14	15	16	17	18	19	20

SUN	MON	TUE	WED	THU	FRI	SAT	SUN
21	22	23	24	25	26	27	28

MARCH

MON	TUE	WED	THU	FRI	SAT	SUN	MON	TUE	WED	THU	FRI	SAT	SUN	MON	TUE	WED	THU	FRI	SAT
1	2	3	4	5	6	7	8	9	10	11	12	13	14	15	16	17	18	19	20

SUN	MON	TUE	WED	THU	FRI	SAT	SUN	MON	TUE	WED
21	22	23	24	25	26	27	28	29	30	31

Ehrenberg, as we have noted above, suggests that columns of figures should be organized vertically. Table 10/3 could in fact have been better organized by putting the data for males above that for females (to match readers' expectations) and by presenting the total entry beneath that of the entry for the males and females (to match normal mathematical expectations). Bartram (1984), however, has shown that bus timetables are better understood when the route listings are placed horizontally across the top of the timetable than when they are placed vertically. Bartram considers that this horizontal listing more clearly reflects the notion of a journey going in a particular direction.

Of course such deliberations do not take into account printing practice. Tables are usually designed by printers to fit particular column widths. It would be difficult to re-orient Tables 10/9 and 10/10, for instance, because the length of the town entries exceeds that of the food entries. This difficulty could be overcome by printing the names of the towns vertically – but this is not a recommended practice.

Guidelines

Some specific guidelines for constructing tables are as follows:

- Make a rough draft first in planning tables. A square grid underlay will be especially helpful. Start from the left.

- Use space systematically to indicate which blocks of material go together.

- If the table is wide and contains many columns, then row headings can be placed both to the left and the right to help comprehension (see Table 10/10).

- If the columns are lengthy then use regular line-spacing (about every five items), as this helps retrieval (see Table 10/10).

- If there are many rows and columns, then space can be saved by numbering or lettering them. However, it is best, if at all possible, to avoid the use of numerous columns and rows, and consequent footnotes.

- If the tables are numbered use arabic numerals rather than roman ones.

- Write a clear but complete title.

- Test out tables with appropriate learners to see what happens when they are asked to use them.

Graphs

In 1979 the US National Institute of Education issued a request for a proposal for research into the presentation and comprehension of graphical displays. The introduction to the proposal made the following observations:
'These visual displays of information are an important means of communication and have become tools for thinking in all scientific and technical fields . . . Recent technological advances in computer graphics suggest that both students and ordinary citizens will be confronted with increasing demands on their ability to comprehend information from graphs and charts . . . Unfortunately, the technological advances in producing graphs and charts have not been accompanied by any significant amount of research about people's comprehension of the displays which are produced.'

Most of the research available on how children and adults understand graphs is of the comparison kind. For example, a typical question might be: 'Is a line graph better than a bar chart?' I have posed the question in this way to suggest that the answer depends in part upon the requirements of the reader. The findings from research of this kind are complex and need teasing out carefully. The papers by Macdonald-Ross (1977), and the text by Tufte (1983) are essential reading for anyone undertaking research in this area. I have drawn some (probably over-simple) conclusions in the next few paragraphs.

It is often thought that the simplest kinds of graph, and the easiest to understand, are line graphs and bar charts. This assumption may be true, but it depends upon the type of information being sought. Line graphs are probably better than bar charts or tables for showing trends. Tables are probably better than line graphs for showing exact quantities.

Bar charts can be subdivided, but such compound bar charts (as they are called) can be confusing (see Figure 10/1). The clarity of bar charts can be improved by putting gaps between the bars.

Figure 10/1

Some different ways of presenting the same information.

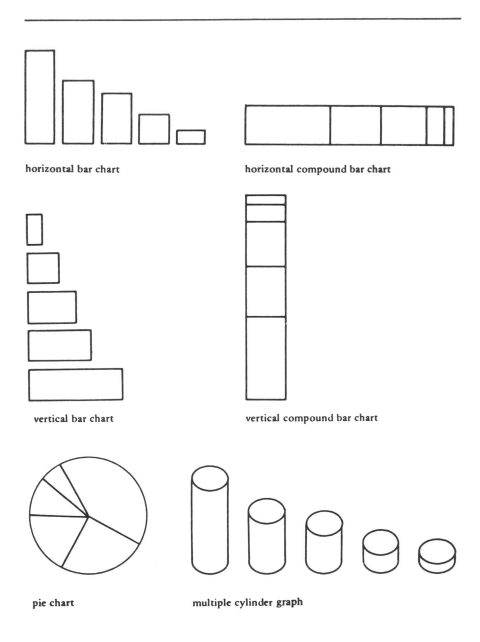

horizontal bar chart

horizontal compound bar chart

vertical bar chart

vertical compound bar chart

pie chart

multiple cylinder graph

Pie charts are said to be easy to understand, but they may also be misleading. It is difficult to judge the proportions accurately when the segments are small. It is also difficult to put the lettering in clearly. Pie charts give a general impression of quantitative relationships but, compared with bar charts, subtle differences are more difficult to detect. Quantitative differences are more readily discernible in bar charts because they are based on multiples of a square module or a regular unit of two-dimensional space.

Pie charts are also difficult to understand if charts with different diameters are being compared. One possible reason for this is that in order to make a circle (or a square) look twice as large, the large one has to be drawn almost four times the size of the small one.

For the same general reason, when the task of the reader is to estimate percentages and quantities, bar charts are better methods of presentation than are cross-sections of three-dimensional objects, such as spheres, cubes, and blocks of columns. (Figure 11/1 illustrates this point in the following chapter on diagrams.)

The aim of a graph is to communicate results easily and clearly. As the vertical and horizontal scales on graphs can be stretched or compressed in order to make points more forcefully, learners need to be made aware of such a strategy. Figure 10/2 shows the effects of such design decisions. Tufte (1983) devotes two whole chapters to the problems of graphical integrity.

Figure 10/2

The same data plotted with different vertical axes.

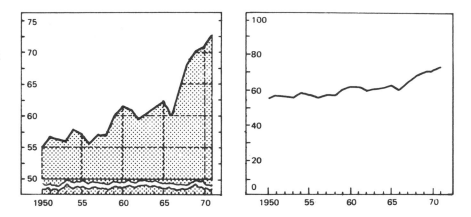

Guidelines

Some specific guidelines for constructing graphs are as follows:

• Keep graphs simple. Use line graphs or bar charts where possible.

• Make a rough draft first to get the sizes in proportion and to see how much space you need: do not cramp graphs in. Use a planning grid and start from the left.

• If the aim of a graph is to compare different conditions then several lines can be plotted on the same graph. However, if more than two or three lines are presented this can be confusing, and it is probably best to separate the lines by typographic cues (eg different symbols or colours) or to use separate graphs. If possible, label the lines on a line graph directly, rather than use a key.

• Letter horizontally both the vertical and the horizontal axes if space permits. It is sometimes helpful to put actual numbers on the sides of the bars in a vertical bar chart or on the top of the bars in a horizontal one.

• Avoid footnotes if possible.

• Write a clear but complete title.

• Test out the graph with appropriate learners to see what happens when they are asked to use it.

Chapter 11   Diagrams, charts and symbols

This chapter considers diagrams, charts and symbols as ways of presenting quantitative information. It is noted that it is pointless to expect children to understand the conventions of such presentation methods (including tables and graphs) without instruction.

While tables and graphs have attracted a great deal of research attention there appears to have been very little published on diagrams, charts and symbols. This appears to be the case despite the fact that there has also been an increase in the use of these devices to present factual data. Most of the research on diagrams is today conducted in the context of work on illustrations. Some features that are not often found in illustrations, however, are cross-sections and plans, and the use of labels or 'call-outs' (in American terminology).

The research shows that children and adults have difficulties in interpreting complex diagrams, particularly of the 'cross-sectional' and 'flow-process' kind. Clearly considerable sophistication would be necessary to follow the process chart of the sort depicted in Figure 11/1. This chart was designed to attract people and motivate them to listen to a broadcast and, therefore, it did not have to be strictly accurate in its presentation. None the less, there are alarming variations in the scales of measurement used.

Jones *et al* (1984) argue that many diagrams are difficult to understand because there is no underlying organization to their labels. Often the reader has no idea where to start reading the labels or where to go in moving from one label to another. Jones *et al* argue that labels should be chunked. Chunking involves grouping related labels under appropriate headings (see Figure 11/2) which, according to them, has a marked effect upon comprehension and recall.

Curran (1978) reported a study of labels or call-outs. He investigated, among other things:
1. The number of call-outs on two technical illustrations.
2. The sequence of call-outs: they were either in a sequential or random order in the illustrations.
3. The way the call-outs were presented: this could be
    *   by name
    *   by number and accompanying reference list
    *   by name and number
    *   by a circled number.

Navy personnel were required (i) to locate parts on the diagram given the call-out name or number, and (ii) to identify parts marked on the diagram. The results suggested that circling the call-out number had little effect, and so too did placing both the name and the number of the call-out on the diagram. The actual number of call-outs made little difference to search times when the call-outs were presented by numbers in a sequential order. However, as the number of call-outs increased from 10 to 62, search time increased by a factor of three or four when the call-outs were presented in a random sequence. Curran thus suggests that if there are more than ten call-outs it is better to number them in sequence.

Figure 11/1

A complex cross-sectional and flow diagram designed to show the process of a typhoid epidemic in Aberdeen in 1964. (Figure © Howard Dyke/*Radio Times*. Reproduced with permission.)

Outbreak tells the story of the 1964 Aberdeen typhoid epidemic

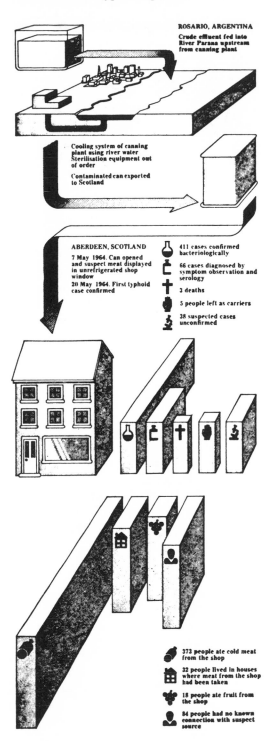

99

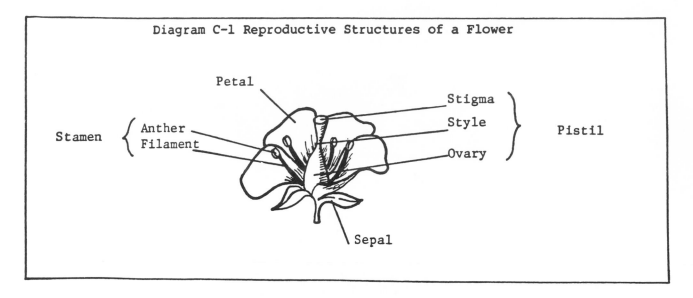

Figure 11/2

A diagram with grouped or 'chunked' labels.

The guidelines listed above for the construction of tables and graphs can also be applied to the construction of charts and diagrams. Again the emphasis should be on simplicity and clarity. Tufte (1983) bemoans what he calls *chart junk* – unnecessary elaborations – which can only confuse the learner. Tufte's text provides the best discussion yet on these matters (complete with guidelines).

Symbols

In Figure 11/1 symbols are used to label items in the chart. The function of a symbol is to communicate without words unambiguously the meaning of the symbol. In Figure 11/1 it is not completely necessary for the symbols to do this because these symbols have captions. However, if symbols are used without captions then this can present problems (see Figure 11/3).

Figure 11/3

These symbols, without captions, are difficult to understand. They actually mean:
1. Hand hot, medium wash
2. Do not bleach
3. Do not iron, dry naturally
4. May be dry cleaned
5. Do not dry clean.

In fact, it seems likely that there are very few symbols that are unambiguous. Indeed, many symbols in current usage only work because of their verbal labels. I was surprised to find, for instance, that more than 50 per cent of a group of British secondary schoolchildren that I tested in 1970 did not understand the meanings of over half of the British traffic signs. Such findings suggest that the meanings of many symbols are not immediately obvious, and have to be learned.

It is interesting to note that in attempts to standardize international public information symbols (eg in airports, railway terminals, etc) it is the verbal label that is standardized rather than the symbol (Zwaga and Easterby, 1984). Attempts are then made to design symbols which will convey this verbal label unequivocally – but different countries are allowed to adopt their own symbols as appropriate.

The isotype system

One set of ideas which uses symbols to present quantitative information is Otto Neurath's *isotype* system. The word isotype stands for 'international system of typographic picture education'. Neurath saw the need to establish a set of internationally agreed conventions in order to make the communication of quantitative information easier and more effective. Some examples of the conventions he established are:

1. A sign or symbol should be used to represent a *certain number* of things, and a greater number of symbols a greater number of these things. (A problem arises here when fractions need to be displayed.)

2. The symbols should be the same size and should be spaced equally; some basic symbols can be combined.

3. Under normal circumstances the time scale of a chart should be presented on the vertical axis, and amounts and quantities on the horizontal one. Charts should be read from top to bottom, and from left to right, thus preserving the eye movements natural to prose reading.

4. Perspective should not be used. When things need to be shown in three dimensions then models or isometric drawings should be used.

Other rules and conventions were listed by Neurath in his text *International Picture Language* (such as standard symbols and colours) but the rules were subject to the idea that they could be modified in the light of experience. The overall consideration was to design something that worked and something that looked attractive. Figure 11/5 shows a typical isotype diagram from one of many children's texts designed by Marie Neurath.

Figure 11/4

An isotype diagram from Neurath, M. (1965) *Living With One Another*. London: Max Parrish. Reproduced with permission of the author.

Europe's Growing Density

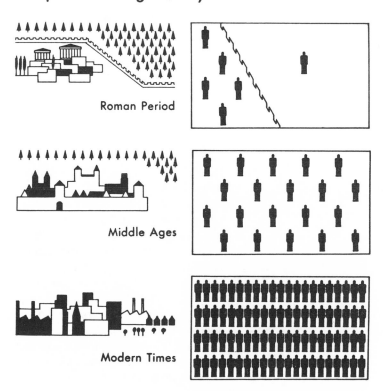

Roman Period

Middle Ages

Modern Times

Each man symbol represents 5 million people

Concluding comments

Macdonald-Ross (1977) concluded his review of the presentation of quantitative data as follows:

> 'No one graphic format is universally superior to all others, though some are so unsatisfactory that they can be virtually discarded from the armoury. To choose the best format for a particular occasion one must decide: What kind of data is to be shown? What teaching points need to be made? What will the learner do with the data? Can previous models be copied? Do we have the time and the skills to execute the format? . . . It pays to remember that graphic communication is an *art*, that is, a skill which results from knowledge and practice.'

Commercial artists as such are not necessarily the best people to employ to make graphical aids, for features such as these require a knowledge of and a respect for standardized signs and drawing conventions, as well as a knowledge of legibility features. Much labelling is rendered illegible by the improper and unskilled use of transfer lettering (see Figure 11/5). These techniques are useful but they are more difficult to use than is sometimes supposed. Certainly, no one without a knowledge of lettering or of legibility requirements should be allowed to use transfer lettering for the making of headings and labelling diagrams. It is far better to tell the printer what is required, and to have him or her provide examples.

Figure 11/5

Transfer lettering is frequently used in the preparation of artwork for instructional text. Although apparently easy to apply, great care needs to be used to ensure the proper spacing of character groups. The current fashion for very close character spacing does not aid legibility, especially when the information has to be taken in at a glance.

educational

educational

The labelling of diagrams and charts should not confuse the drawing, either through positioning or by the careless placing of lines which connect the label to its referent. Indeed, in designing instructional text graphical aids to comprehension need as much care and thought in their making and positioning as do other parts of the text. In fact, the rational planning of material cannot properly begin until the nature, function and dimensions of such components have been decided on, and decided *prior to actual production*.

As a general rule, illustrations and graphical aids should be positioned to follow statements made in the text. To use such features merely to decorate the page, or to 'make it look more interesting' degrades the value of these methods. It is poor design practice to force either the graphical components to conform to unsuitable column widths or the text to conform to the spatial demands of the graphical components.

Other factors which limit the legibility of graphical aids are:

1. Words set at an angle from the horizontal.

2. Reversed lettering, that is, white characters on a black or a strong or dark-coloured background.

3. Show-through, that is, the appearance on the page of the lines or drawings printed on the reverse side. (Current British Standard documents are printed on a paper having a substance of 73 grammes per square metre which seems satisfactory.)

Finally, in considering the use of graphical aids, we should note that it is obviously pointless to expect children to understand them automatically. Unless the conventions are taught, as reading and writing are taught, graphical aids can have little value in instructional materials.

Summary

1. **Children – and many adults – do not automatically understand the conventions used in graphical and tabular aids. The more complex the data being presented the more likely this is to be so.**

2. **Tables, graphs, diagrams, charts and symbols all benefit from being kept simple. The typography of such graphical aids should have a high standard of legibility. Poorly designed graphical aids present extra difficulties.**

3. **The positioning of graphical aids requires careful planning in advance of production. Such materials should not be positioned on a 'let's put this here' basis, but related to the content of the text.**

Chapter 12   Forms

This chapter discusses the layout and content of forms. Attention is drawn to the costs of completing and processing badly designed forms, and to the need for a progressive cycle of testing in order to eliminate difficulties when producing forms. The impact of new technology on form design is briefly considered.

Research on the design of forms has accelerated in the last ten years or so. The impetus for this has come from two main sources – notably Plain English campaigns in the USA and the UK – and recognition by government that something needs to be done to reduce the number of forms available and their related costs.

The Rayner review of British government forms attempted to estimate the number of forms in use in the UK in 1981. The review estimated that the number of different external forms – those issued to the public or business – was about 38,000, and that the number of internal administrative forms was about double this number. The total number of different government forms was estimated at well over 100,000. If standard letters and explanatory leaflets are added to this total the final sum must be incredible.

Similar numbers have been reported in the United States. The Associated Press estimated that in the mid-1970s the US government issued some 98,000 different kinds of form per year, and received over 50 million responses. The Internal Revenue Service alone sent out over 3,500 different forms per year.

In attempting to estimate the cost of forms, researchers have distinguished between the costs of *processing* a form and the costs of *producing* it. Most investigators consider that the main costs lie in the processing of forms and, indeed, it has been suggested that the cost of processing forms exceeds the cost of producing forms by a factor of 2 to 3. The Rayner review estimated (on the basis of 10p per form) that the processing cost of British government forms and leaflets was in the area of £200 million a year (in 1981). One extreme example quoted in the review illustrates the difference between processing and production costs: in this case it was estimated that one form cost £4 to process and 3p to print.

One additional figure which is not so easy to assess is the cost to the user of badly designed forms. Poor forms take a long time to complete and they can lead to errors and mistakes. These can result in users failing to obtain certain advantages or even – in extreme cases – being prosecuted for giving false information. Errors made on forms usually lead to greater processing time and forms often have to be returned for correction – thus starting the cycle again. Some government forms have startling error rates: Waller (1984) reports that the old British P1 income tax form had an error rate of 84 per cent.

Findings such as these (in both the UK and the USA) prompted governments to set up form review bodies, to scrutinize the forms in use, to see how many could be disposed of, and to see which forms needed drastic attention quickly. The results of these initiatives have led to dramatic improvements in some of the forms issued by the Inland Revenue and the Department of Health and Social Security in the UK, and by the Internal Revenue Service in the USA (see Figures 12/1a and 12/1b).

What are the features of forms that cause problems?

Patricia Wright (1981, 1984) suggests that three main areas need to be considered in form design. These are:
1. The overall layout.
2. The content: the questions themselves and the kind of responses that are required.
3. The adjunct material: instructions, tables, footnotes, etc.

Supplementary benefit

Please come in and see us about supplementary benefit on

_____ **at** _____

Please come in on time. If you are late, we may not be able to give you a new time on the same day.

When you come in, please go to the waiting room. Wait till your name is called out.

If you cannot come in at the right time, ring up and tell us. The number is at the bottom of this letter.

Please read the list on the back of this letter. We need to see the things on it to work out your benefit. If you forget to bring them, it could hold up your benefit.

Please turn over

Social Security Office
Government House
137 Bennett Road
Anytown AN1 6XX.

● Phone 738833

A165 in E
Date

Figure 12/1b

A revised version of the same form.
(Reproduced with permission of Chrissie Maher.)

DEPARTMENT OF HEALTH AND SOCIAL SECURITY

(LO address) Davenport House, Hulme Place,
The Crescent,
Salford. M5 4PA

Tel 061-736 5888 Ext 204 ....

Ref No 5810/............... 19

Mr /Mrs /Miss ....
....
....

Your appointment is

on .... (Date) at .... (Time)

PLEASE ARRIVE AT THE OFFICE PROMPTLY AS IT MAY BE DIFFICULT TO FIT IN ANOTHER APPOINTMENT THE SAME DAY IF YOU ARRIVE LATE. Do not wait to see the receptionist but go straight to the waiting room until you are called for interview at Booth number ....

What you need to bring with you

SO THAT YOUR PROPER ENTITLEMENT TO SUPPLE-MENTARY BENEFIT CAN BE DECIDED YOU MUST PROVIDE EVIDENCE ABOUT YOUR CIRCUMSTANCES. YOU SHOULD THEREFORE BRING ANY OF THE FOLLOWING ITEMS YOU HAVE FOR YOURSELF, YOUR WIFE, OR ANY DEPENDANTS:-

Form B1 or B1C from the Unemployment Benefit Office if unemployed (unless already submitted).

Last two wage slips.

Letter from employer if holding a week's wages in hand.

Please turn over

Form A 165
(_Erw EW 56F_)

Figure 12/1a

The original layout for a DHSS supplementary benefit form.

The layout of forms

The design principles advocated in the early chapters of this text apply, of course, to the design of forms. Forms, however, are often exceptional because of their complexity. Waller (1984) lists, for instance, the following typical items on a government form:

- Form title
- Form code number
- Initial instructions
- Part headings
- 'Write clearly' and similar reminders
- Primary questions
- Supplementary questions
- Question qualifier/explanations
- Tick boxes and their labels
- Response space labels
- Special notes next to response spaces to deal with typical errors predicted by pre-testing
- Conditional user directions ('if you ticked *yes* . . . ')
- 'For office use' area
- Page break guides ('(section name) continued', 'Now please turn the page' etc)
- Declaration

It is clear that systematic spacing in the text is required to help the user to deal with such complexity. A basic grid, as an underlying guide to organization, is essential. ISO paper sizes (particularly A4) should be employed to meet the requirements of metrication and the move towards standardization. To recapitulate, such rationalization should lead to a reduction in printers' overheads, to less wastage, and to easier storage. Furthermore, standard page-sizes will fit into the ISO standard envelope styles which are POP (Post Office preferred). The minimum size of these envelopes is 90 mm x 140 mm, the maximum 120 mm x 235 mm.

One interesting layout problem discussed by Wright is that there are often differences between peoples' estimates of the difficulty of a form, and how easy or difficult it actually is for them to complete it. Wright suggests that if people anticipate that a form is going to be difficult to fill in, then this may lead to procrastination or the form not being completed at all. This kind of problem also arises with lengthy forms. A study by Rucker and Arbaugh (1979) showed how two factors (attractiveness and length) can interact. They reduced a 21-page questionnaire to three pages by using a matrix rather than a list format (see below). However, the three-page matrix format looked more difficult and led to significantly fewer questionnaires being returned.

It is perhaps worth remarking at this stage that attempts by form designers to get as much text as possible on to small sheets of paper may be counter-productive (as we saw in Example 4 in Chapter 5). The cost-effectiveness of forms and questionnaires depends upon them being completed accurately and returned.

The language and logic of forms

The general points made in Chapter 6 about writing instructional text apply to the writing of forms – only more so. The main difficulty, commmented on by many researchers, is that form designers do not seem to consider the language, the logic and the layout of forms from the user's perspective. If the sequence of questions is constrained by the needs of the administrator then the logic of the form may seem unnatural to the user. The users' expectations of what they will be asked next may make them misread subsequent questions, or lead them to give additional information which is irrelevant or out of context.

The language of forms can present especial difficulties. Examples of gobbledegook abound, and there is no need to repeat them here. We know from everyday experience that difficulties confront us all in understanding government forms, but perhaps the greatest difficulties are faced by the less able and by speakers of limited language ability. Consider, for example, this piece of text from a form provided by the US Immigration and Naturalization Service:

> 'If you are the spouse or unmarried minor child of a person who has been granted preference classification by the Immigration and Naturalization Service or has applied for preference classification, and you are claiming the same preference classification, or if you are claiming special immigrant classification as the spouse or unmarried child of a minister of religion who has been accorded or is seeking classification as a special immigrant, submit the following . . .'

One way of helping form designers with such problems has been to provide them with a thesaurus of alternative expressions which are more easily understood by the general public than the kind of text shown in this example. The British Department of Health and Social Security's *The Good Forms Guide* contains such a thesaurus, and an abbreviated version of this has been printed as an appendix to this chapter.

Asking questions

Wright points out that one special difficulty with the content of forms lies in the variety of ways in which questions can be asked and in which answers can be given. Common deficiencies (listed by Lefrere *et al*, 1983) include questions which:

- are ambiguous
- are unintelligible
- ask too much at once
- limit respondents' ability to provide the required information (by too narrow a range of response options and/or too little space for answers)
- ask for information of a kind that may be provided more readily in some other way (from departmental sources or through an interview)
- yield answers that cannot be easily processed by clerks
- provide unwanted information.

Figure 12/2 shows the mess that can ensue when a variety of methods of questioning and answering are used on a single form. Figure 12/2 shows *six* different methods being used. Research has not fully established whether or not any one particular method is preferable to another – they all have advantages and limitations, as we shall see. From the point of view of consistency and ease of completion, however, it might be helpful if form designers could keep to one or two methods of questioning within a single form.

Figure 12/2

This form asks the reader to respond in six different ways. (Figure reproduced with permission from Patricia Wright.)

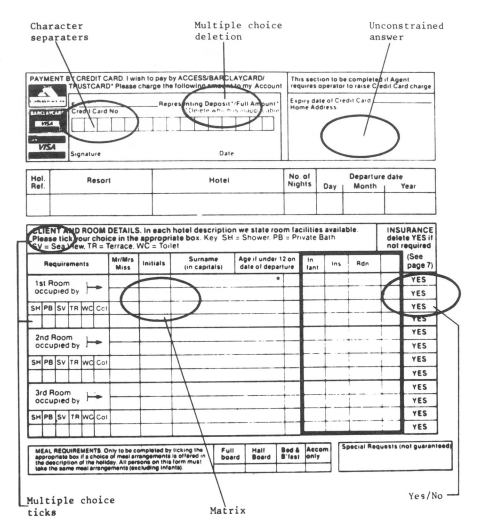

The little research that has been done with these methods suggests the following:

- *Character separators*

  1.
  2.
  3.
  4.

  Studies have shown that writing one letter per box in a framework such as framework 2 takes users more time and the result is less legible than writing in frameworks 3 and 4. Framework 1, surprisingly, produces the worst results and framework 4 the best. Typing answers in constrained boxes can also cause difficulties. (Forms seldom state whether 10 pitch or 12 pitch should be used.) And often the horizontal and vertical spacing of the form does not match that of the typewriter.

- *Unconstrained answers*

  Often insufficient space is left for unconstrained answers. If your name is Fred Smith you can just fit it in this amount of space
  What would you do, however, if your name was Madeleine Woodward-Waters? Answer spaces need to be big enough to fit the answer in, and they need to be located alongside the question being asked so that users know just where they are supposed to write. One should avoid the tendency (which often arises with justified composition) of having the answer space a long way from the end of the question.

- *Matrix formats*

  In matrix formats the reader has to refer to information presented in both columns and rows, and this can impose memory problems. The problems are increased when the number of rows and columns is more than three and when respondents have to use coded letters to indicate their reply (eg 'Give name of school if attending. Write D if dependant (see note D), P if of personable age (see note E), SB if receiving supplementary benefit.') Studies indicate that matrix formats can be resdesigned in ways that markedly reduce memory loads, thus improving their effectiveness.

- *Multiple-choice questions*

  With multiple-choice questions respondents have to indicate which choice is most appropriate for them. This can be achieved by a variety of methods, none of which is entirely satisfactory. Deletions can cause difficulties especially when negatives are concerned (eg 'Delete what does *not* apply'). Ticking a particular choice usually causes less difficulty especially when positive responses are appropriate (eg 'Tick which applies to you'). However, many people use ☑ or ☒ interchangeably and it is not clear whether ☒ means NO or YES. As noted above, multiple-choice formats can cause additional difficulties when two or more pieces of information have to be combined in order to answer a question in a matrix format.

- *Yes/no answers*

  This form of answer is perhaps the most simple, but this simplicity is perhaps deceptive. Respondents find it easier to answer questions that lead to the answer *yes* rather than to the answer *no*. Furthermore, questions demanding yes/no answers are often ambiguous, especially when there are two or more related parts. Wright provides an example of the question 'Are you over 21 and under 65?' which gave particular difficulties to senior citizens who answered each part in turn.

It is curious how many things can be ambiguous. In a form used at Keele by job applicants, for example, the respondent was asked at one point: 'Give previous experience with dates'. One candidate for a lecturer's post replied, 'Moderately successful in the past, but I am now happily married!'. In this example all that was required to remove the ambiguity was an additional comma: 'Give previous experience, with dates'. Factors such as these suggest the need for careful pre-testing of individual questions (and indeed whole forms) with small groups of appropriate respondents in order to eliminate such difficulties.

Unfortunately, the problems posed by asking questions on forms are multiplied when the forms present different kinds of questions; questions in sequence; questions which may be omitted; and questions which may lead to different outcomes or branches. As Waller (1984) remarks, the problems of sequencing are:

- *Linguistic* – questions and instructions must be clearly understood.
- *Logical* – branches must be organized to achieve the most economical flow.
- *Graphic* – the designer must display the pathway through the form clearly so that all the irrelevant questions are skipped and all the relevant ones answered.

Adjunct materials

In addition to the main content of the form there are the adjunct materials – the instructions, the footnotes, the guides to completion, and 'the small print'.

An excess of instruction on how to complete a form or questionnaire can be confusing, especially if this is printed in small type. Indeed, many readers just ignore the small print. It may be better, therefore, (as with the current income tax form) to refer the reader – where appropriate – to separate notes. (This does not mean, of course, that the notes should be printed in small type, or in government jargon!) Another useful alternative is to use a wide left-hand margin, and to place notes here, opposite the item to be completed.

Wright points out that the initial instructions on how to complete a form can make great demands on the memory processes of form fillers. She says that expecting form fillers to remember the minutiae of such instructions seems over optimistic. No doubt reminders can be placed strategically throughout the form but, of course, the better the form the less that is required in the way of explanation of how it is to be completed.

Designing forms: case-histories

Studies of form design tend to fall into two main categories: those that compare revised forms with their original versions, and those that describe how research techniques can be applied when new forms are required.

Comparison studies

A number of studies have been reported which have compared original with revised forms – the revisions being based on what research has suggested concerning linguistic and typographic features. Most of these studies, but not all of them, have had successful outcomes.

Mullarky (1976) redesigned two forms involved in guard and gun licensing procedures for the Florida State Department in America. The problems here were not so much concerned with redesigning the wording of the text (although this was important) but with redesigning (i) the way in which the forms could be folded to fit inside standard size envelopes, and (ii) the way in which they could be filed by the State Department. Mullarky's solution to these problems resulted in a reduction of $800 in labour and materials on the first run of 50,000 copies and a change from legal-size to letter-size envelopes and filing. This led to a 20 per cent reduction in filing space requirements, a 25 per cent reduction in floor loading, and a gaining of the equivalent of five miles of paper.

Felker and Rose (1981) tested a revised version of the US government's Federal Communications Commission form concerning the use of two-way radios on recreational boats. Groups of experienced and inexperienced boat users were given either the old or the new forms and asked to complete the same test questions on information contained in the rules. The results showed that the new rules were significantly easier to use and to understand. People using the revised rules answered the test questions more quickly, more correctly, and were significantly better at identifying appropriate rules. The form fillers also rated the revised rules easier to use.

Firth (1981) studied the redesign of five forms and letters produced by the British Department of Health and Social Security, comparing the originals with the revised forms. The results showed improvements in readability and attractiveness for four forms and improvements in office effectiveness for three of them. Firth concluded that forms could be redesigned at a superficial level with a great deal of success: they could be made to look brighter, more attractive, and easier to read. However, Firth argued, it was much harder to achieve success at improving comprehension and reducing errors. To achieve successful results Firth recommended the procedure of testing the first draft of the form with appropriate respondents, revising on the basis of the results obtained, retesting and revising again until all the difficulties were removed.

Designing new forms

The test-revise-test-again model was used extensively in a study reported by Lefrere *et al* (1983) and Waller (1984). These reports describe how colleagues at the Open University set about producing a form to be used by unemployed people claiming supplementary benefit in the UK.

A prototype form had been developed and piloted by the Department of Health and Social Security. The form was small in format (165 mm x 204 mm) with eight pages organized as a folded concertina. (Illustrations of this form, and its various revisions are provided in the reports.) Although the respondents found the form attractive to look at, they found it difficult to use. About 75 per cent of the completed forms were unsatisfactory in one way or another – leading to forms being returned and/or respondents being followed up in some way before an assessment of benefit could be made.

The main sources of error in the prototype form appeared to be:
- Problems of relevance and contextual interpretation: the form did not elicit enough information for an assessment to be made, and appeared irrelevant to a large number of claimants;
- Problems of reading sequence: many sections did not apply to many claimants, but the form gave inadequate directions concerning which parts were to be completed;
- Problems in graphic design: poor design practice also contributed to the problems of sequencing.

The problems of the form ranged from the fairly obvious to the subtle and the debatable.

In order to redesign the form the prototype was first tested with small groups of appropriate respondents. (Interestingly, part of this assessment included the use of a reading-recorder to assess which pieces of text were read and in what order.) The aim of this first assessment was to isolate the main causes of difficulty, and to collect data against which the redesigned forms could later be compared. It appeared from this first testing that the form was not asking the right questions to gather the information that the civil servants needed. In addition, many questions were ambiguous.

Thus a redesigned version was prepared. The emphasis in this redesign was on revising the language and on sequencing the form: thus the content was well spaced and simply designed so that the confusions brought about by poor design practice (noted earlier) could be avoided at this stage. The revisions focused on making the branching instructions more explicit, and in giving users clearer instructions when they first encountered such a branching instruction.

This redesigned version was tested (again with small groups of appropriate respondents). It was clear that improvements had been made, but that more could be done. So a third version was then prepared. Headings for the different sections were added, and the routing instructions were further improved.

The testing of this third version showed that this had solved most of the problems. Thus a fourth and final version was prepared. This version used colour coding for the main headings (earlier versions had been in black and white), a larger page-size (200 mm x 330 mm) and yet another resequenced order. Now, once the logical and linguistic problems had been sorted out, typographical considerations could be brought to the fore.

This final version was tested with larger groups of appropriate respondents. The results now indicated that only about 25 per cent of the forms were completed unsatisfactorily (as opposed to the original 75 per cent). Today, after further revisions, the successful completion rate is estimated to be over 80 per cent. These impressive results have led to massive cost benefits for the Department of Health and Social Security.

The reports by Lefrere *et al* (1983) and Waller (1984) provide much more detail than I am able to give here. Lefrere *et al* conclude with a list of guidelines which they produced to serve the special needs of the British DHSS Forms Unit. Some of these guidelines are as follows:

- We recommend the use of simple, straightforward language in forms, so far as this is possible.
- We recommend that the needs of the applicants should prevail wherever possible, and that the sequence of questions should be that which is most natural from the point of view of the person filling in the form.
- We recommend that no decision to change a form's format should be taken before tests of the proposed new version are conducted.
- We recommend that standard formats be drawn up for recurring circumstances. This could lead to the development of a house style for families of forms (ie forms of similar function).
- We recommend that each major section on a form should be numbered and titled. Both number and title should be used in routing instructions. Questions within a section should normally be un-numbered, and signalled visually using bullets or some similar device. Reference numbers or letters meant for clerical use should not intrude on the reading area reserved for the applicant.
- We recommend the use of sufficiently different weights of type to ensure a clear distinction between main questions and subsidiary questions. Lower-case should be used for questions, with the first letter in upper-case.
- We recommend the use of such devices as screens or rules to differentiate the instructions on a form from the spaces for reply.
- We recommend that the Forms Unit should arrange for the regular testing of the more important and novel forms on small representative groups of potential users; and that large-scale evaluations be conducted from time to time to check on the continued reliability and validity of the small-scale testing method.

New technology and form design

The requirements of automatic data-processing have had a marked effect on the design of forms and questionnaires but probably not for the better as far as users are concerned. The development of optical scanners has led to a significant increase in the use of formats which employ multiple-choice rather than open-ended questions. Furthermore, in order to speed up data-processing, coded answers often have to be entered on to another separate sheet. Sometimes, for example, each of the multiple-choice alternatives is given a number and questions are answered by writing down the numbers chosen on a separate response sheet. In even more complicated situations more than one answer may be permitted, the possible combinations are all given numbers, and it is the choice of one of these numbers that has to be recorded elsewhere. (Such a system is used by several examining boards in the UK.) The result of all this seems to be unnecessarily complicated for the user. Indeed Wright cites evidence which shows that such complex response requirements lead to an increase in errors.

Much automatic data-processing (both input and output) ignores the basic rules of typographic design expressed in this textbook. In particular much computer-generated text is in all-capital letters, and teleprinters do not seem to be programmed to take account of the structural requirements of the text. Consequently such materials are often difficult to use.

One advance that we may expect, however, is the development of interactive forms displayed on visual display units (VDUs). This particular advance is to be welcomed because it will allow questions to be posed one at a time and the sequencing of the questions to depend upon the response given to individual items. Such automated sequencing will remove one of the major problems of form design. Undoubtedly computer-assisted form filling will present additional problems – users will have to be able to operate computer terminals. Also some traditional problems – how to phrase the questions – will remain.

But maybe computer-assisted writing will aid even here. If, for example, the research described in Chapter 6 on computer-aided writing is applied to form design, then material such as the Department of Health and Social Security's thesaurus of easier expressions (see appendix to this chapter) could be utilized to guide form writers on the appropriateness of their questions. It may also be the case, one day, that guides about the best ways of asking particular questions and presenting them on screens or paper might be stored in order to help form designers with their task. Designers will be able to call up different formats, choose between alternatives, and produce different versions easily for testing.

Summary

1. **Poorly designed forms are costly for users and costly for their originators. They take longer to fill in, they produce more errors and they take longer to process.**

2. **Three areas of difficulty in form design lie in the overall layout, the content and the adjunct material.**

3. An attractive layout is likely to help response rates: a form that looks difficult to complete may lead to procrastination or no response at all.

4. The style and wording of forms needs to be simple, clear and appropriate to the user.

5. The ways of writing questions and the ways of asking for responses are many and varied. It would seem helpful to try to limit particular forms in this respect.

6. Comparison studies show that forms can be redesigned and improved on the basis of what is known about linguistics and typography. One valuable approach to testing new forms (or revised versions of old ones) is to test, revise, retest and revise again until the objective of accurate completion is achieved.

7. Forms and questions which are designed for automatic data-processing often cause difficulties for respondents because of this. Interactive computer-assisted form filling, however, offers useful advantages, and so will computer-aided writing and design.

Appendix to Chapter 12. Simpler wording

The list below of abstract and simpler terms is a shortened version of the thesaurus of abstract terms presented in *The Good Forms Guide* published by the British Department of Health and Social Security. It is reproduced with permission of the DHSS and the authors, David Lewis and Jane Castor-Perry.

A fuller, updated and revised list is currently in use at the DHSS. Enquiries should be addressed to David Lewis, The Forms Unit, DHSS, 6 St Andrews Street, London EC4 3AD.

Readers are reminded that the list contains only suggestions and that the alternative terms will not be appropriate in every case.

Commonly used words and phrases with some alternatives to choose from

accede to – agree
accompanying – with
accordingly – so
acquaint – say; tell
acquire – get
adequate – enough
adjustments – changes
advantageous – useful; helpful; better
advise – say; tell
affected – made a difference; changed
aggravated – made worse
alternatives – choices; others
anticipate – expect
apparent – clear; obvious
appropriate – right; proper
approximately – roughly; about

begin – start
on behalf of – for
beneficial – useful; helpful

calculate – work out
in case of – if
cease – finish; stop
commence – begin; start
complete – fill in
component – part
conceal – hide
concerning – about
in connection with – about
consecutive – following on
as a consequence of – because
consider – think

construct – make
consult – talk to; see; meet; ask
convenient – suitable

decrease – make less
defer – put off; delay
delete – cross out
demonstrate – prove; show
denote – show; be
desire – want
diminish – lessen
disclose – tell; show
discontinue – stop; end
dispose – get rid of
distinguish – show; point out
duration – time

economical – cheap
eligible – can get; have the right to get
employment – job; work
enable – allow
to enable us – so that we can
enclosed – inside; with
endeavour – try
enquire – ask
ensure – make sure
entitled to x – have the right to (get) x
equivalent – equal; the same
erroneous – wrong; false
estimate – work out
exceptionally – only when; in this case
excessive – too much
excluding – apart from; not including
exclusively – only
expect – think

facilitate – help
feasible – possible
foot of the page – bottom
for the purpose of – to
to forward – to send

generally – usually
on the grounds that – because

henceforth – from now on
hereby – now
herein – here
heretofore – until now
herewith – now
however – but

immediately – now; at once
to implement – to carry out; do
in as much as – because
in case of – if; if there is
in connection with – about; for

in excess of – more than
in lieu of – instead of
in order to – to; so that
in respect of – about
in the course of – while; during
in the event – if
in the neighbourhood – near; about
in the near future – soon
incapable – cannot
incapacitated – unable to work
income – money that you have coming in
independent – not part of
indication – sign
individual – one; person; you
infirmity – illness
inform – say; tell
initiate – start; begin
inspect – look at; check
irrespective of – whether or not; even if
it is felt that – I/we feel/think
it is suggested that – I/we suggest

liable to – have to; may have to
locate – find

maintain – keep; look after
maintenance – keep; upkeep; looking after; care
mandatory – must
marginal – small
maximum – the most
minimum – the least
miscellaneous – other
modify – change

necessary – must
necessitate – need; require
negligent – not taking enough care
nevertheless – but
notify – tell
notwithstanding – even though
numerous – many

obligation – duty
obsolete – out of date
obtain – get
occupation – job; work
occur – happen
option – choice
otherwise – if not
overleaf – on the other side of this page

particulars – details; facts
payable – may/can be paid; can be cashed
pending – until
performed – did
permit – let
come into possession of – get

practically – almost; nearly
prescribed – set; fixed
prior to – before
proceed – go
procure – get
profession – job; work
prolonged – for a long time
promptly – quickly
provided that – if; as long as
purchase – buy

qualifying (period) – the time that matters
quote – say; give

re – about
in receipt of – get; getting
receive – get
reconsider – think again
recoverable – get back; which we can get back
redeemable – can be used; can be cashed
with reference to – about
in regard to – about
regarding – about
regulation – rule
relevant – is important; matters
remedy – cure; answer
remuneration – pay
report – tell
represents – shows; stands for; is
request – ask
require – need
reside – live
residence – where you live; home; house
in respect of – about; for
restriction – limit
resuming – starting again
retain – keep
retention – keeping
return – send (back)
revenue – income; money coming in
revise – alter

select – choose
settlement – payment
signature – sign here
so far as . . . is concerned – about
space is not sufficient – there is not enough room
state – say; tell us; write down
statement – information about; details of
statutory – legal; by law; set down by law
straightaway – now; as soon as it happens; as soon
as you can; at once
submit – send
subsequently – later
subsidized – helped
sufficient – enough
supplementary – extra; more

tenant – person who pays rent
terminate – stop; end
therefore – so
to date – so far; up to today
together with – and
transform – change; alter
transmit – send
transpire – happen

ultimately – in the end; at last
unable – cannot
undertake – agree to
utilize – use

verification – proof
vocation – job
voluntary – by choice

whether – if
wholly – all; completely; fully
with a view to – to
with reference to/with regard to – about

Chapter 13

Listed information: contents pages, references, bibliographies and indexes

Some texts consist of lists of items – with main and sub-elements recurring. Some lists are simple, like contents pages, and some more complex, like bibliographies. This chapter examines the role of spatial and typographical cueing in the presentation of such lists and comments on the influence of new technologies on their design and preparation.

Some forms of text consist of what might be termed 'lists' or 'strings' of material, much of which is often computer-generated. Some mailing lists, for instance, contain hundreds of entries, all of which can be divided into sub-elements – names, street numbers, towns, counties and postal codes. Likewise references, bibliographies, and indexes usually contain a large number of entries, all of which contain a number of sub-elements. Two problems for the designer here are (i) how to present this material economically, and (ii) how, at the same time, to make it easy to use.

Lists are scanned rather than read word for word, but detailed reading does take place when an appropriate entry is found. Readers scan down lists (and across in multi-column formats). Designers generally make use of a judicious mixture of typographic and spatial cues in order to facilitate scanning and the retrieval of different sub-elements. The difficulty for the designer is, as ever, to avoid the over-use of cueing (which seems to be prevalent in many printed materials), and to avoid its under-use (which could lead to materials being difficult, if not impossible, to use). Unfortunately there has been little research in this area to assess the cost-effectiveness of the many possible solutions to these problems.

Contents pages

Contents pages provide relatively straightforward list structures. In books it is usual to provide simply a chapter number, a title, and a page reference. In academic journals the situation is a little more complex. Contents lists here also contain the names of the authors as well as the titles of the articles and their page numbers. (In addition there is usually ancillary material describing the title of the journal, its date and volume number, and other display matter such as editorial addresses and subscription rates.)

Although journal contents pages present fairly simple list structures, one has only to scan the journals on library shelves to see the variety of solutions adopted by designers for presenting such lists to the reader. In fact designing journal contents pages appears to encapsulate almost all of the general problems of typographic decision making. Some of the relevant questions are as follows:

- How is the contents page to be used? What size is it to be? Where is it to be positioned?
- How can the structure of the material be conveyed clearly on a page of this size?
- How many different cues must be used to give appropriate emphasis to each of the different elements in the list?
- Will these cues be readily understood by the reader?
- How can one evaluate the appropriateness of the decisions made?

There have been few studies evaluating such design decisions but I must claim responsibility for three of them. In 1980 I published two studies on users' preferences for different layouts of journal contents pages, and in 1981 (with Corina Guile) I published a third.

In the 1980 studies I set out to compare readers' preferences for several layouts (32 in all). Sixteen of these layouts distinguished the name of the author as a sub-element in the list by using a typographic cue – namely by printing it in italic: the remaining 16 layouts were exactly the same as the first 16 but without the italic cue.

The 16 designs (with or without italic cue) fell into three groups:
- main elements grouped horizontally
- main elements grouped vertically
- names and titles run together.

The following example shows how the same reference might appear in each of these three main styles:

Horizontal grouping

M.A. Ayoub.   Optimum design of containers for
                              manual material handling tasks.   67

Vertical grouping

M.A. Ayoub.
Optimum design of containers for
manual material handling tasks.   67

Run-on

M.A. Ayoub. Optimum design of containers for
manual material handling tasks.   67

Experienced journal readers were asked to make systematic comparisons between all 32 designs using the method of paired comparisons. This involves each judge systematically comparing layout 1 with layout 2 and stating a preference, then layout 1 with layout 3 and stating a preference, then layout 1 with layout 4 and so on . . . When all the comparisons have been made with layout 1, the judge then starts again and systematically compares layout 2 with all the subsequent layouts, and then layout 3 with all the subsequent layouts, and so on. What is scored is the number of times a particular layout is preferred over the others.

The results of these enquiries showed that:

1. Readers significantly preferred the horizontally grouped designs to the vertically grouped ones, and these in turn were significantly preferred to the run-on ones.

2. Each of the versions with a typographic cue was preferred to its equivalent version without it.

The three most preferred designs (all variations on horizontal grouping with typographic cueing) are shown in Figure 13/1.

These studies showed that the spatial arrangement of the contents page was the primary determinant of its preference ranking, and that the presence of a typographic cue enhanced the preferences for a particular layout. The horizontally grouped layouts were the most preferred because they enabled the readers to use the page in different ways. As one of my judges put it, 'If I am looking to see if X has a paper, then I want to scan the names; if I am browsing through journals to see if there is a topic of interest to me, then I need to skim through the titles; if I am hunting for a specific article, then I need to find the author'. Some judges were strong adherents of the view that the readers need to see the titles first: others that the authors were more important. The advantage of the method of horizontal grouping is that it allows readers with such different preferences to look at whatever they want first.

Figure 13/1

The three most preferred settings for contents pages.

M. A. Ayoub	67	Optimum design of containers for material handling tasks.
R. J. Phillips and Liza Noyes	73	Searching for names in two city street maps.
H. Saltik and J. S. Ward	79	A study of ergonomic factors in washbasin design.
J. Pilitsis and G. P. Redding	87	The use of performance profiles in the design of a systematic medical suturing training programme.
Alison R. Goodwin, Susan Thomas and J. Hartley	93	Are some parts larger than others? Qualifying Hammerton's quantifiers.

M. A. Ayoub	Optimum design of containers for manual material handling tasks.	67
R. J. Phillips and Liza Noyes	Searching for names in two city street maps.	73
H. Saltik and J. S. Ward	A study of ergonomic factors in washbasin design.	79
J. Pilitsis and G. P. Redding	The use of performance profiles in the design of a systematic medical suturing training programme.	87
Alison R. Goodwin, Susan Thomas and J. Hartley	Are some parts larger than others? Qualifying Hammerton's quantifiers.	93

Optimum design of containers for manual material handling tasks.	M. A. Ayoub	67
Searching for names in two city street maps.	R. J. Phillips and Liza Noyes	73
A study of ergonomics factors in washbasin design.	H. Saltik and J. S. Ward	79
The use of performance profiles in the design of a systematic medical suturing training programme.	J. Pilitsis and G. P. Redding	87
Are some parts larger than others? Qualifying Hammerton's quantifiers.	Alison R. Goodwin, Susan Thomas and J. Hartley	93

In 1981 Corina Guile and I were able to extend these findings further: we replicated the main conclusions described above, this time using university students as participants and using contents pages which varied the lengths of the article titles and the numbers of authors for each article. In this study we thus found support for horizontal grouping with several different kinds of contents page.

One final feature of contents pages that deserves mention here is that concerning the position of page numbers. It is a common practice in many contents pages – because of the notion of justification – to have the text begin on the left-hand side and the page numbers to be aligned on the right. This practice sometimes leads to large gaps between the text and the page numbers.

References

References present slightly more complex list structures than contents pages: now we have to consider not only the authors and the titles of the articles, but also the date and place of publication. In addition there are conventions for referencing book titles, journal articles, articles in edited collections and so on. (See British Standards 1629 and 5605.)

Different journals use different procedures to indicate the main and sub-elements within reference lists. Most use run-on procedures although some use a spatial arrangement.

In 1979 my colleagues and I reported our findings from a study on the presentation of references which was very similar in design to those which I have just described concerning contents pages. In this reference study we asked experienced readers to compare 12 sets of references. Six sets were presented with typographic cues to indicate where the entry could be found (ie italic was used for book or journal titles and volume numbers) and six were presented without the typographic cues. The references were set in two main styles as follows:

Vertically grouped
Dennis, I. (1975)
The design and experimental testing of a hospital
drug labelling system.
Programmed Learning & Educational Technology, 12, 2, 88-94.

Run-on
Dennis, I. (1975) The design and experimental testing of a hospital drug labelling system. *Programmed Learning & Educational Technology, 12*, 2, 88-94.

The readers were required to state their preferences for the 12 sets of references again using the method of paired comparisons. The results obtained were very similar to those obtained with the contents pages:

1. Readers significantly preferred the vertical grouping arrangement to the (more usual) run-on presentation.

2. Each of the versions with typographic cueing was preferred to its equivalent version without it.

The most preferred setting was that shown in Figure 13/2.

Again the spatial arrangement of the list was the primary determinant of its preference ranking, and the presence of the typographic cues only enhanced the preferences for a particular layout.

The experiments described above relied on preference measures. They did not consider whether or not vertical grouping would help readers to find information in the list more easily than would a run-on reference list. Unfortunately I have been unable to detect any published papers on the effectiveness of searching reference lists printed in different ways.

Figure 13/2

The most preferred setting for journal references.

Allan, M.D. (1957)
    Training in perceptual skills.
    Occupational Psychology, *31*, 113-119.

Annett, J. (1961)
    The role of knowledge of results in learning: A survey.
    NAVTRADEVCEN Technical Report No 342-3,
    US Naval Training Device Center, New York.

Annett, J. (1969)
    Feedback and Human Behaviour.
    Harmondsworth: Penguin.

Annett, J., and Duncan, K.D. (1967)
    Task analysis and training design.
    Occupational Psychology, *41*, 211-221.

Chaney, F.B., and Teel, T.S. (1967)
    Improving inspector performance through training and
    visual aids.
    Journal of Applied Psychology, *51*, 311-315.

Drury, C.G., and Fox, J.G. (eds) (1975)
    Human Reliability In Quality Control.
    London: Taylor and Francis.

Embrey, D.E. (1976)
    Signal detection theory in the analysis and optimisation
    of industrial inspection tasks.
    Unpublished PhD thesis, University of Aston in Birmingham.

Gibson, E.G. (1953)
    Improvement in perceptual judgements as a function
    of controlled practice or training.
    Psychological Bulletin, *50*, 401-431.

Mackie, R.R., and Harabedian, A. (1964)
    A study of simulation requirements for sonar operator
    trainees.
    Technical Report No 1320-1, US Naval Training Device
    Center.

Sinclair, M.A. (1979)
    The use of performance measures on individual examiners
    in inspection schemes.
    Applied Ergonomics, *10*, 17-25.

Finally in this section I must return to the issue of cost-effectiveness. Table 13/1 shows my estimates of the amount of extra space required for vertically grouped references with different column widths.

Table 13/1 The number of extra lines required for vertically grouped reference systems in different column widths.

	No. of columns and widths	No. of lines for six run-on references	No. of lines for six vertically grouped references	Average number of extra lines per reference
Journal A	1 x 135 mm	10	20	2.0
Journal B	2 x 67 mm	20	26	1.3
Journal C	3 x 50 mm	23	26	1.1

Table 13/1 shows that it might be much more costly to use a vertically grouped system in a single-column setting. However, the actual costs will depend on other factors. Journal A in Table 13/1, for example, starts new articles on a fresh right-hand page so there is room for manoeuvre here. Journal B starts new articles on the next full page (whether it is on the left- or right-hand side) so there is limited extra space here. Journal C, however, runs the articles straight on after each other (sometimes on the same page), so there is no additional space in this journal. Also, since Journal C prints over 50,000 copies a month, extra pages in this journal would be very costly.

Thus, summarizing the research described in this section, it appears that readers prefer vertically grouped references, but that they are less economical in terms of space than traditional run-on ones. However, if attractiveness is deemed important, then vertical grouping is recommended. Readers may judge for themselves the value of such a decision when they turn to the bibliography of this text.

Bibliographies

A typical bibliography might contain a list of entries ordered alphabetically by the author, with each entry, for example, containing five sub-elements – the author's surname and initials, the title of the work, the publisher, the price, and the ISBN classification number. There are, of course, many different ways of presenting such a list structure. These ways are fewer if one is working with typewritten composition, but even here the use of space, capitals, and underlining can achieve much to distinguish the separate elements in each entry. With printed versions more typographic variants are available, eg different typefaces and different weights.

In 1974 Herbert Spencer and his colleagues compared ten different systems of presenting typewritten bibliographic material (see Figure 13/3). With one exception (system 4 which required the use of bold type) all the systems could be prepared on a standard office typewriter or on an upper- and lower-case line printer. Students in each condition were required to underline the given price of a book from a list of 12 randomly chosen authors. The experimenters recorded the number completed in a period of 45 seconds.

The results indicated that the three best systems were systems 7, 9 and 10 in that order. This suggests that the most effective coding systems are those which make a clear distinction between successive entries, and between the first word of each entry and the rest of the entry. In fact, system 7 is also the most practical since it is more economical in terms of space than systems 9 and 10.

Spencer *et al* followed up this study with a further experiment published in 1975. In this study they used printed rather than typewritten bibliographic materials and thus they were able to examine more closely the advantages and disadvantages of the spatial and typographic cueing of entries. The materials they used are shown in Figure 13/4 in a reduced size. In this experiment students were required to do two tasks: (i) search for authors (for 45 seconds), and (ii) search for titles (for one minute and 45 seconds).

Figure 13/3

The ten coding systems compared by Spencer *et al*. (Figure reproduced with permission of Herbert Spencer.)

System 1

PAGE, MICHAEL FITZGERALD. FORTUNES OF WAR. HALE. £1.90.
823.91F (B72-10444) ISBN 0 7091 2803 7
PALLAS, NORVIN. CODE GAMES. STERLING; DISTRIBUTED BY WARD
LOCK. £1.05. 001.5436 (B72-09950) ISBN 0 7061 2328 x

System 2

Allman, Michael. Geological laboratory techniques.
Blanford Press. £8.50. 550.28 (B72-17338) ISBN 0 7137 0559 0
Allsop, Kenneth. Adventure lit their star. Revised ed.
Penguin. £0.35. 823.91F (B72-17562) ISBN 0 14 003446 3

System 3

HAIGH, Basil. Organic chemistry of nucleic acids. Part A.
Plenum Press. £9.00. 547.596 (B72-10819) ISBN 0 306 37531 1
HAINING, Peter. The Channel Islands. Revised ed. New
English Library. £1.50. 914.2340485 (B72-12211)

System 4

Barrett, Edward Joseph. Essentials of organic chemistry.
Holt, Rinehart and Winston. £5.00. 547 (B72-17335)
ISBN 0 03 080348 9
Barrow, Charles Clement. A short history of the S.

System 5

Bartlett, Kathleen. Lovers in Autumn. Hale. £1.30. 823.91F
(B72-10379) ISBN 0 7091 2329 9
Bassett, Michael Gwyn. Catalogue of type, figured & cited
fossils in the National Museum of Wales. National Museum

System 6

-Cartland, Barbara. A ghost in Monte Carlo. Arrow Books
Ltd. £0.25. 823.91F (B72-12081) ISBN 0 09 906180 5
-Cartwright, Frederick Fox. Disease and history. Hart-Davis.
£2.50. 904.5 (B72-11136) ISBN 0 246 10537 2

System 7

Edson, John Thomas. Wagons to Backsight. Hale. £1.10.
823.91F (B72-10401) ISBN 0 7091 2394 9
Efemey, Raymond. The story of the parish church of St
Thomas, Dudley. 5th ed. British Publishing. Unpriced.

System 8

Cadell, Elizabeth. Bridal array. White Lion Publishers
Ltd. £1.80. 823.91F (B72-17578) ISBN 0 85617 622 2
Cafferty, Bernard. Spassky's 100 best games. Batsford.
£2.50. 794.159 (B72-16145) ISBN 0 7134 0362 4

System 9

Manessier, Alfred. Manessier. Adams and Dart. £10.50.
759.4 (B72-10983) ISBN 0 239 00098 6
Mangalam, J J. Mountain families in transition: a case
study of Appalachian migration. Pennsylvania State

System 10

FARNHAM, Ann. Action mathematics. 5. Cassell. £0.65. (non-net)
372.73045 (B72-15925) ISBN 0 304 93803 3
FARQUHAR, Ronald M. The earth's age and geochronology.
Pergamon. £2.50. 551.701 (B72-17343) ISBN 0 08 016387 4

The results showed that when searching for authors, spatial coding proved a more effective variable than typographic coding. However, when searching for titles, then typographic coding was more important than spatial coding. Spencer *et al* concluded their article by recommending Style 2C or Style 5C as the best – the argument being that these compromise styles allow good results whichever task is being performed. In short, they concluded that the best design depends upon the use to which the material will be put.

Figure 13/4

The 18 coding systems for bibliographic material compared by Spencer *et al*. (Figure reproduced with permission of Herbert Spencer.)

1. Copy runs on. 3 space units between each entry.

2. 1st element of each entry begins a new line. 2nd, 3rd and 4th elements run on.

3. All elements begin a new line.

4. All elements begin a new line. 1st element of each entry full out. 2nd, 3rd and 4th elements successively indented.

5. Line space between entries. 2nd, 3rd and 4th elements run on.

6. Line space between entries. Each element begins a new line.

A.
(1) Roman caps & lowercase
(2) Roman caps & lowercase
(3) Roman caps & lowercase
(4) Roman numerals

B.
(1) Roman caps
(2) Italic caps & lowercase
(3) Roman caps & lowercase
(4) Italic numerals

C.
(1) Italic caps & lowercase
(2) Bold caps & lowercase
(3) Roman caps & lowercase
(4) Italic numerals

ISBN 0 85292 069 5. Bajin, Boris, Olympic gymnastics for men and women. Prentice-Hall £5.50. 796.41 ISBN 0 13 633925 5. Baker, C. D. Lepard's metric reckoner: for cost per thousand sheets given price per kilogramme and weight in kilogrammes. Pitman. £4.00. 338.4367620942 ISBN 0 273 25242 9. Baldwin, Brenda. Skid prevention and control. R. W. Noon. £0.30. 629.283 ISBN 0 95032394 0 2. Ball, Alan. Alan Ball's international soccer annual No. 4. Pelham. £1.00.

Pettman, Dorothy. Oral embryology and microscopic anatomy: a textbook for students in dental hygiene. 5th ed. Lea and Febiger; Kimpton. £3.80. 611.314 ISBN 0 8121 0376 9. Philips, Francis Edward. Greek philosophical terms: a historical lexicon. New York University Press; University of London Press. £3.80. 180 ISBN 0 340 09412 5. Piatek, Clare Gray. Perspectives in surgery. Lea and Febiger; Kimpton. £9.45. 617 ISBN 0 8121 0279 7.

Learmouth, Peter. The houses we build. Central Committee for the Architectural Advisory Panels. £0.25. 721.0942 ISBN 0 95073012 0 0. Leary, Harold W. The PL/1 machine: an introduction to programming. Addison-Wesley. £5.60. 001.6424 ISBN 0 201 05275 x.

Emmet, Louis Emanuel. Emmet's notes on perusing titles and practical conveyancing. 2nd (cumulative) supplement. 15th ed. Oyez. £3.00. 346.420438 ISBN 0 85120 124 5. Emsden, Leo. Sound of the sea. White Lion Publishers Ltd. £1.80. 823.91F ISBN 0 85617 894 2.

Fincher, Norah M. Mingling, and other poems. Stockwell.

Fielding, A. J. Internal migration in England and Wales: a presentation and interpretation of 'city-region' data. Centre for Environmental Studies. £0.50. 301.3260942 ISBN 0 901350 52 4.

Figes, Eva. Konek landing. Panther. £0.35. 823.91F ISBN 0 586 03638 5.

Serrailier, Ian. The clashing rocks: the story of Jason and the Argonauts. Carousel Books. £0.20. 823.911 ISBN 0 552 52022 5.

Seuffert, Muir. Devil at the door. Hale. £1.40. 823.91F ISBN 0 7091 2907 6.

Hutchinson and Co. (Publishers) Ltd. £6.00. 230.01 ISBN 0 09 108850 x. WALTERS, PATRICK GORDON. *The Cabinet.-Revised ed.* Heinemann Educational. £1.00. 354.4205 ISBN 0 435 83915 2. WALTON, BRUCE. *Augusta Whittal; Sir Robert Peel.* Constable. £3.25. 942.081 0924 ISBN 0 09 458290 4. WARD, WILLIAM F. *Electronics testing and measurement.* Macmillan. £4.50. 621.381 ISBN 0 333 12544 4. WARNATH, ARTHUR WILLIAM.

GILL, JOHN. *The tenant.* Collins. £1.50. 823.91 F: ISBN 0 00 221843 7. GILLARD, R D. *Essays in chemistry, Vol 3: 1972.* Academic Press. £1.80. 540 ISBN 0 12 124103 3. GILLEN, LUCY. *Dangerous stranger.* Mills and Boon. £0.80. 823.91F ISBN 0 263 05021 1. GILLESPIE, IAN ERSKINE. *Gastroenterology: an integrated course.* Churchill Livingstone. £1.50. 616.3 ISBN 0 443 00854 0.

SALT, JOHN. *Parents - participation and persuasion in primary education.* University of Sheffield Institute of Education. £0.15. 372.1103 ISBN 0 902831 07 0. SANDERS, ED. *The family: the story of Charles Manson's dune buggy attack battalion.* Hart-Davis. £2.50. 301.4494 ISBN 0 246 10528 3.

MELLISH, E MUDGE. *Rust and rot and what you can do about them.* Angus and Robertson. £1.25. 520.11223 ISBN 0 207 95436 4. MENDELSOHN, JACOB. *Decision and organization: a volume in honor of Jacob Marschak.* North-Holland Publishing. Unpriced. 330.1 ISBN 0 7204 3313 4.

BAKER, HILARY. *Oakes Park, Sheffield: the historic home of the Bagshawe family since the year 1699.* English Life Publications. £0.15. 914.2746 ISBN 0 85101 057 1.

BALDWIN, CECIL HENRY. *Teaching science to the ordinary pupil. 2nd ed.* University of London Press. £3.45. 507.12 ISBN 0 340 15583 3.

BALL, GEORGE SAYERS. *Who is a white-collar*

CERVINE, JO. *X-Ray diagnosis positioning manual.* Glencoe Press; Collier-Macmillan. £1.50. 616.07572 ISBN 0 02 4733270 2.

CHADWICK, ANGELA. *The infernal desire machines of Doctor Hoffman: a novel.* Hart-Davis. £1.95. 823.91F ISBN 0 246 10545 3.

Bristol and Gloucestershire. Darwen Finlayson. £3.20. 914.241 ISBN 0 85208 065 4. *Ramchand, Kenneth. The West Indian novel and its background.* Faber and Faber Ltd. £1.70. 823.009 ISBN 0 571 10139 9. *Ramsay, Anna Augusta Whittal; Sir Robert Peel.* Constable. £3.25. 942.081 0924 ISBN 0 09 458290 4. *Randall, Christine; Collier; Macmillan. £1.05. 745.54 ISBN 0 02 767190 9. *Ranis, Gustav. The gap between rich and poor nations:*

Perraton, Jean. Urban systems: collection and management of data for a complex model. University of Cambridge Department of Architecture. Unpriced. 301.36094229 ISBN 0 902248 29 8. *Perry, Eric Akers. The Parish Church of Holy Trinity, Wickwar. New ed.* British Publishing. Unpriced. 914.241 ISBN 0 7140 0677 7. *Perryman, Albert Charles. Life at Brighton locomotive works, 1928-1936.* Oakwood Press. £0.90. 625.261

Hindmarch, Jack. Urban systems: Multiple choice questions for intermediate economics. Macmillan. £0.50. 330.076 ISBN 0 333 13570 9. *Hislop, George. Let history judge: the origins and consequences of Stalinism.* Macmillan. £5.75. 947.08420924 ISBN 0 333 13409 5.

Medlen, Wolf. The Samson riddle: an essay and a play, with the text of the original story of Samson. Vallentine, Mitchell and Co. Ltd. £2.25. 822.914 ISBN 0 85303 152 5. *Mehmet, George Byron. A.B.C.'s of transistors, 2nd ed. reprinted.* Foulsham. £1.25. 621.381528 ISBN 0 572 00579 2.

Adams, Arlon T. Topics in intersystem electromagnetic compatibility. Holt, Rinehart and Winston. £12.00. 621.38411 ISBN 0 03 085342 7.

Adeney, Carol. This morning with God: a daily devotional guide for your quiet time. Vol. 1. Hodder and Stoughton. £0.40. 242.2 ISBN 0 340 15997 9.

Atkins, Arthur William Hope. Moral values and political

Chamberlain, Peter. German army semi-tracked vehicles, 1939-45. Model and Allied Publications. £0.40. 623.747 ISBN 0 85344 136 7.

Chance, June F. Applications of a social learning theory of personality. Holt, Rinehart and Winston. £6.05. 155.2 ISBN 0 03 081810 0.

Similar experiments to these were reported by Spencer and Reynolds concerning the design of computer output microfilm (COM) catalogues for presentation by microfiche or microfilm. In their 1976 paper Spencer and Reynolds summarized what research had been done on reading and using microfilm and made suggestions about needs for the future.

Perhaps at this point it would be useful to have some definitions. A *microform* is any form, either film or paper, which contains images too small to be read with the naked eye. Microforms on paper are now so rare that the term microform has become almost synonymous with *microfilm*. A *microfilm reader* is a device used to magnify the images on the microfilm. Most readers are designed for use with one type of microfilm, eg roll film or microfiche. A *microfiche* consists of a piece of film (usually 6 x 4 inches) that can contain images of over 250 pages of A4-sized text. Microfilms and microfiche were traditionally produced by photographing documents, but in recent years computer output has been put directly on to film to produce *computer output microfilm* (COM).

Spencer and Reynolds reported that COM was becoming increasingly popular as a form of computer output for a variety of structured texts, such as customer accounts, stock records, parts lists, price lists, hotel reservations, book lists, library catalogues, etc. Its advantages lie in its compact nature; its disadvantages lie in its use.

In most cases the users of COM are involved in brief search tasks rather than in continuous reading – although browsing may occur. Because of these requirements, the spatial arrangement of the text is very important. Unfortunately, COM layouts are often determined by computer programmers who try to minimize the bulk of their computer output by making a maximum use of the 132 characters per line and the six lines per inch that are available on most line printers. Reynolds (1979) provides some horrendous examples.

In 1979, Reynolds and Spencer presented the results of two experiments. These were concerned with evaluating different COM layouts:
1. by manipulating the intercolumn spacing of tabular materials, and
2. by comparing a single- versus a double-column format when the presentation was in a cine-mode (vertical roll) or a comic-strip mode (horizontal roll).

In experiment (1) they found that increases in the column spacing were accompanied by increases in the time taken to search the material. In experiment (2) they found overall that the double-column format was better than the single-column one, and that the cine-mode was better than the comic-mode. However, these results were specific to the user's task. When the test involved a lot of searching *within* individual elements, then the double-column format was better; however, when the test involved much searching *for* the actual elements in the first place, as well as within them, then the single-column format was better. These results, then, are not unlike those one might expect from experiments with conventionally printed materials. Spacing is important, but so, too, are the requirements of the user.

In their discussion, Reynolds and Spencer make the point that is frequently made by researchers in the new media. They say that the layout of COM is often inappropriately modelled on the layout of conventional text. Their point is that when you change from one medium to another you might require a different layout to suit the limitations and the possibilities of the new technique.

Indexes

A number of texts recommend how to design an index but the majority of these are concerned with explaining how to compile an index rather than how to present one. One exception is the British Standards Document 3700 *Recommendations for the Preparation of Indexes* (1976). This pamphlet provides probably the clearest specification available for the typographic design of a textbook index.

A good index is easily defined, but difficult to achieve. A good index lists in detail the contents of a book in alphabetical order, showing clearly the main items and – by cross-referencing – the interrelationships between them. The problems for the indexer concern the amount of detail allowed and the level of structure to be shown. Some indexes are extremely complex in terms of levels, and the designer's use of indentation seems to defy immediate comprehension (see Figure 13/5).

Figure 13/5

An example of complex indentation in an index from a statistics textbook.

```
Median test, extension of, for k indepen-
            dent samples, method, 179-184
        example, 180-184
      power-efficiency, 184
       .compared with Kruskal-Wallis
         test, 193
  for two independent samples, 111-116
    compared with other tests for two
      independent samples, 156-158
    function, 111
    method, 111-115
      example, 112-115
    power, compared with Kolmogorov-
        Smirnov two-sample test, 136
      compared with Mann-Whitney
        U test, 123
    power-efficiency,115
    rationale, 111-112
Meeker, M., 24n.
Minimax principle, 8n.
```

Indexers and authors disagree about who best constructs an index. The Society of Indexers resolutely refuses to accept that authors can make good indexers: 'An author,' they say, 'lacks the skill and the objective distance to index his or her own book.' Some authors, on the other hand, say just the opposite: 'An author knows best his or her own book and is best qualified to index its ideas and concerns.' There is probably some truth in both of these assertions. Authors may have been with their materials too long for them to appreciate the ways in which naive readers might want to search their texts: and an indexer, on the other hand, might not appreciate the background experience of readers in specialist disciplines (different from that of the indexer).

One might perhaps have more faith in the judgement of the Society of Indexers if there was agreement between professional indexers on how to index particular texts. Unfortunately there is not: different indexers index differently (Jones, 1983).

Inspection of indexes published before the 1976 British Standards Document leads one to the conclusion that up to that date there appeared to be no agreed method of layout – apart from alphabetical listing. Indeed, even here there was (and there still is) debate: some authors recommend alphabetic listing *letter-by-letter* and others recommend alphabetic listing *word-by-word*. These different organizations have advantages and disadvantages and can lead to quite different sequences. For example:

letter-by-letter	*word-by-word*
music	music
musicality	music case
music case	music copying
music copying	musicality

One line of research here (which can be profitably extended) has been to look at how children and university students order words for indexes, and how they search indexes printed in different sequences. In 1981 my colleagues and I asked a group of 195 12-year-olds and a group of 27 university students to put sets of words 'in the order they would expect to find them in a book's index'. We found that 85 per cent of the children used a letter-by-letter technique and none used the word-by-word technique. On the other hand, only eight (30 per cent) of the students used the letter-by-letter technique and only four (15 per cent) the word-by-word technique. The students preferred to group words according to their meaning rather than to their spelling: 12 (45 per cent) did this – producing inconsistent orders. Such findings suggest that adults might have greater difficulty using indexes than young children. Adults have more elaborate concepts and these elaborations might not match those provided by an indexer.

Gordon (1983) advocates that all children's information books should contain an index, and that children should be taught how to use indexes in the primary school. Approximately 60 per cent of children's reference books contain indexes although Gordon thinks that they are not always too well done. Indeed, in nine children's textbooks that I examined in 1976, I found nine different layouts for the index. The most common variations seemed to lie in the choice of column structure (one, two or three columns), the use of centred or left-ranging layouts, the positioning of key letters if they were provided, the use of capital or lower-case letters for each entry, the use of typographic cues to convey sub-entries (eg italic, lower-case or smaller typesizes), the alphabetical or chronological ordering of sub-items (or indeed both in history texts), and the amount of indentation used to convey (i) sub-items, (ii) carry-overs in the list of sub-items, and (iii) additional carry-over problems when page turning was involved.

Assessing the design of indexes

There have been one or two attempts to carry out comparison studies between different layouts of indexes, and to assess the effectiveness of different styles of indexes in actual working situations.

Keen (1976) compared six published indexes for Unesco in the field of library information science. He used seven measures with his searchers (library science students) as follows:

- Ability to find the relevant source documents.
- Ability to find documents judged by the searchers to be relevant.
- Ability to suppress perceived irrelevant documents.
- Search time.
- Search effort (page turns).
- Intelligibility of the index entries.
- Subjective preferences.

The results, discussed in detail by Keen, indicated that three indexes (*Library and Information Science Abstracts*, *Library Literature*, and *Information Science Abstracts*) were much better on most of these measures than were the remaining three others (*Computer and Control Abstracts, Bulletin Signalétique,* and *Referativnyi Zhurnal*), but that it was not really possible to make distinctions within the first three.

Bowman *et al* (1983) reported how readers at IBM used indexes in a variety of computer manuals. They concluded that formatting was very important. Readers spent less time and made fewer mistakes when the index had:

- Indented entries.
- Large letters dividing each alphabetical section.
- Multiple entries and cross-references for the same procedure.

Burnhill *et al* (1977) compared the effectiveness of the three layouts shown in Figure 13/6. These layouts were as follows:

Style 1.   A balanced approach, with page numbers ranged right.
Style 2.   A left-ranging approach with each sub-item entered vertically.
Style 3.   A left-ranging approach with sub-items run on.

Style 1 was based on the traditional justified approach to the problem, which is now somewhat rare. Styles 2 and 3 are commonly seen in indexes today.

Approximately 200 children were given a list of items and asked to find and circle as many items as they could in their particular index for a period of five minutes. The results showed no significant differences between the layouts in terms of the number of items circled in each index during that period of time.

It is difficult to generalize the design of all indexes from such a simple study. Nevertheless, there are perhaps certain implications for the design of simple indexes even though the children did not have to generate their own search tasks. The results obtained suggested that style 3 was no worse than style 2 (the closest to the British Standards recommendations). If one had to choose between styles 2 and 3 then the number of sub-items, their length, and the number of pages referred to would all be important considerations. The study by Burnhill *et al* suggests, however (other things being equal), that it might not be necessary to place each sub-item on a new line. Style 3 was best in terms of cost-effectiveness and this, therefore, is the style that I have specified for the printers of this textbook.

Style 1

Flour beetle: see Tribolium
Fluoridation
  investigations 142-3
  objections 143
Fluoride ions 142-3
Fluorine 131
Fly agaric toadstool 32
Food 21, 28
  appearance 85, 86
  cartoon 83
  colouring, artificial 86
  comparison 85, 86
  cost 85, 86
  fresh, compared with
    preserved 85, 86
  preparation 85, 86
  preservatives in 86
  preserved 82-6
  production 141-2
  storage 85
  taste 85, 86
  texture 85
  transport 85
  U.K. consumers expenditure
    chart 84
Force 9, 10, 11
Forces, electrostatic:
  see electrostatic forces

Style 2

Flour beetle: see Tribolium
Fluoridation
  investigations 142-3
  objections 143
Fluoride ions 142-3
Fluorine 131
Fly agaric toadstool 32
Food 21, 28
  appearance 85, 86
  cartoon 83
  colouring, artificial 86
  comparison 85-6
  cost 85, 86
  fresh, compared with preserved
    85-6
  preparation 85, 86
  preservatives in 86
  preserved 82-6
  production 141-2
  storage 85
  taste 85, 86
  testure 85
  transport 85
  U.K. consumers expenditure chart
    84
Force 9, 10, 11
Forces, electrostatic: see
  electrostatic forces

Style 3

Flour beetle: see Tribolium
Fluoridation, investigation 142
  objections 143
Fluoride ions 142-3
Fluorine 131
Fly agaric toadstool 32
Food 21, 28; appearance 85, 86;
  cartoon 83; colouring,
  artificial 86; comparison 85
  cost 85, 86; fresh,
  compared with preserved 85-6;
  preparation 85, 86;
  preservatives in 86;
  preserved 82-6; production
  141-2; storage 85; taste 85,
  texture 85; transport 85;
  U.K. consumers expenditure
  chart 84
Force 9, 10, 11
Forces, electrostatic: see
  electrostatic forces
Forest: coniferous 31; deciduous
  32; evergreen, map 31; photo.
  tropical, map 31
Foucalt 106-7
Fractional distillation 89
Franklin, Benjamin 123, 125
Fresh, Hermann 108-110

Figure 13/6

Extracts from the three styles of index used.

New technology and listed information

The computer revolution has changed dramatically the ease of publication of annual yearbooks, library catalogues, society registers, etc. Wordprocessing facilities allow one to insert, delete, update and modify entries easily. In addition, such systems allow one to re-organize lists alphabetically.

In terms of this chapter the new technology is most applicable to the design and presentation of references, bibliographies and indexes. Computer-assisted indexing programs, for example, are now becoming available as one of the tools of the writer's 'workbench'. Such programs can format entries and sub-entries, arrange them in alphabetical order, assign page references, and update page references when the text is modified or edited. Undoubtedly we may expect the same facilities for the presentation of references and bibliographies.

In the case of indexes it is common to assume that, although wordprocessors will help with their preparation, they will not help with the selection of items – the main problem for indexers. This may be true with current programs. In the future, however, it will undoubtedly be possible to develop programs to produce indexes automatically. Dillon and Macdonald (1983) have already reported one apparently successful attempt in this direction.

Fully automatic indexing is an exciting possibility. Apart from relieving authors of the strain of indexing, it should be possible to manipulate various theoretically designed parameters in order to see which of them leads to more successful indexes.

One final comment may be made here. If the presentation of references, bibliographies and indexes is to become fully automated, then there will be a need for agreed international standards to facilitate the electronic exchange of all this information. When such standards start to materialize I hope that good design practice will not be forgotten.

Summary

1. Listed information presents two problems for the designer: how to present the material economically and how to make it easy to use.

2. Studies of contents pages and references using preference measures suggest that readers find spatial cueing attractive, and that spatial cueing is more important.

3. Studies of references and indexes using search tasks, however, have not, as yet, provided much support for the value of either spatial or typographic cueing.

4. Work with bibliographies – the most complex listed information discussed – does suggest, however, that spatial and typographic cues are both valuable for different purposes.

5. Wordprocessing facilities will greatly assist authors in the preparation of references, bibliographies and indexes.

6. New international standards will be required to facilitate the electronic exchange of this kind of information.

Chapter 14   Designing electronic text

This chapter considers how far the findings of research with printed text can be used in the design of electronic text. Electronic text has certain limitations (particularly in terms of its spacing) and certain advantages (eg animated graphics). It is suggested that electronic text will be easier to use when more attention is paid to the design features discussed in this textbook.

In this chapter the term 'electronic text' is used to cover text on visual display units (VDUs), cathode ray tubes or television screens (CRTs), and printouts of displays from such screens. The aims of this chapter are to consider (i) how far the contents discussed in the earlier chapters (particularly those concerning the legibility, layout, and language of prose) are relevant to electronic text, (ii) how conventionally printed and electronic text differ, and (iii) how these differences can cause problems in using electronic text.

The legibility of text on VDUs and CRTs is a function of several additional factors to those we have considered so far with respect to printed text. Simcox (1983) divides these factors into two kinds: traditional and modern. Traditional factors include parameters such as luminance, contrast, character height, character width, spacing between the characters and so on. Modern factors include such things as flicker, glare, refresh rate, drift, colour, and resolution, as well as parameters related to CRT size and to stroke and dot-matrix technology. Most of these modern factors are not the main concern of this particular text, but some references to studies of their effects are provided in the bibliography.

When considering the legibility of text on VDUs and CRTs it is often assumed that all that we know about the design of printed text can be applied straightforwardly to the design of electronic text. In some respects this is the case: much of what I have discussed in earlier chapters – stressing the need for spatial consistency in layout and for the importance of simple language – is directly applicable to electronic text. For example, it would seem wise, in my view, to opt for unjustified left-ranging text, to avoid word-breaks, and to use consistent horizontal and vertical spacing in the text to separate and group related parts. Clearly, too, in preparing screen-based instructional text, the text needs to be carefully pre-planned using a simple reference grid.

Limitations of screen-based electronic text

However, screen-based electronic text differs from printed text in many ways. So in many instances the assumption that what is true of print is also true of electronic text is (unfortunately) wishful thinking. At the time of writing most electronic text is presented on screens tied to an underlying grid of 24 lines of text and 80 letter spaces, although previously 40 letter spaces were common. The amount of text that one can actually get on to a grid of 24 lines and 40 letter spaces is illustrated in the following paragraph:

We have printed this paragraph in this format to demonstrate the maximum amount of text that could be displayed on a number of machines. The most that could be put on to a line limited to forty characters is shown here. The maximum number of lines one could use at any one time was twenty-four, but only if you did not object to ascenders and descenders touching one another. If you wanted to separate them with a line space, as here, you had only *twelve* usable lines.

A quick calculation shows that it takes about 20 'pages' like this to present the same amount of information that one can see in one double-page spread of this particular textbook.

```
PH OR HISTOGRAM AND STICK IT LIGHTLY (BL
UE TACK/PVC TAPE) ONTO THE GRAPHICS TABL
ET ON TOP OF THE GRID SHEET. TAKE CARE T
O LINE IT UP STRAIGHT - AN A4 SHEET IS B
EST LINED UP WITH THE TOP OF THE FINE GR
ID SECTION.
   2, PUT DISK 19 INTO DRIVE 1 AND SWITCH
 ON THE APPLE. SELECT THE CORRECT PROGRA
M FROM THE MENU.


INPUTTING THE GRAPH - GENERAL
--------------------------------
   1, THE DIFFERENT SECTIONS (AXIS, LINES
, SYMBOLS ETC.) MAY BE DRAWN IN ANY ORDE
R BUT IT IS GENERALLY LESS CONFUSING TO
PUT IN AXES FIRST.
   2, BECAUSE IT IS EASY TO MAKE MISTAKES
 IT IS BETTER TO INPUT COMPLEX GRAPHS IN
 SECTIONS, AND STORE THEM IN SEPARATE FI
LES. THESE MAY THEN BE PLOTTED ONTO THE
SAME SHEET OF PAPER TO REBUILD THE COMPL
+ETE GRAPH. THIS ALSO ALLOWS YOU TO REUS
E THE SAME SET OF AXES WITHOUT INPUTTING
```

Figure 14/1

An early example of electronic text.

Not only is the screen grid constricting in terms of space, but also it is differently arranged from that of a typical textbook page. For example, in this text the information area measures approximately 11.5 cm by 24 cm, whereas a typical screen may measure 20 cm by 15 cm. Unlike most print, screen text is typically wider than it is deep.

This arrangement produces particular problems (as we shall see below). However, it should be mentioned that developments in screen design might well remove some of them. Larger (A4) screen sizes are already available and, indeed, there are even larger split-screen displays with the facilities for inserting footnotes or extra details in additional 'windows' as appropriate.

In this chapter I shall consider three kinds of problem presented by today's small grid configuration. They are:

1. Problems of legibility: often designers attempt too much text per 'page'.

2. Problems of search and retrieval: more attention has to be paid to helping readers to know both where they are and how to find their way to and fro in the text.

3. Problems of writing text to match this particular medium: authors have to try to write grid-sized chunks of text, and they face great difficulties incorporating tabular and graphic materials.

```
STARTING UP.
------------
    1, First draw a rough copy of the graph or
histogram and stick it lightly (Blue Tack/PVC
tape) onto the Graphics Tablet on top of the
grid sheet. Take care to line it up straight -
an A4 sheet is best lined up with the top of
the fine grid section.
    2, Put disk 19 into drive 1 and switch on the
Apple. Select the correct program from the
menu.


INPUTTING THE GRAPH - GENERAL
-----------------------------
    1, The different sections (axis, lines,
symbols etc.) may be drawn in any order but it
is generally less confusing to put in axes
first.
    2, Because it is easy to make mistakes it is
better to input complex graphs in sections, and
store them in separate files. These may then be
plotted onto the same sheet of paper to rebuild
the complete graph. This also allows you to
reuse the same set of axes without inputting
them every time if you have a number of similar
graphs.
```

Figure 14/2

A more modern computer printout version of the same text as that shown in Figure 14/1.

Problems of legibility

Typical problems are presented by poorly designed character sets, and by writers trying to put text on every line on the screen. Figure 14/1 illustrates such problems with an older display system. Technological developments have led to improvements. Figure 14/2, for instance, shows an obvious gain: this is the same text set in a computer printout.

Problems of search and retrieval

It is difficult, if not impossible, to flip through, or skim an electronic text and to make side-by-side comparisons of different pages. You cannot put your finger in an electronic text to keep your place while you check back on an earlier point, although there are developments in this respect. In one British electronic journal it is possible to keep and compare the top few lines of various pages.

Many researchers suggest the use of running headings (as in textbooks) to indicate where one is and numbered paragraphs to aid search and retrieval. Running headings, of course, occupy space – space which is at a premium in electronic text. The use of running headings may mean that only about three-quarters of the screen (or less) remains for the information itself.

Attention also has to be paid to the design of indexes and contents pages to help the users find their way about the text. Such pages list topics and sub-topics with keyboard references, and readers have to select appropriately. It is conventional to structure such 'menus' in a hierarchical or 'tree-like' manner with the basic or primary choices first, and the lower level (or more refined choices) later.

One of the problems here is that choices deemed appropriate by the author may not match what the reader has in mind – making search difficult. The designer has to choose between providing a few detailed (and crowded) menus, or a larger number of less detailed (and less crowded) ones which will take the reader time to work through. It may well be that once readers are familiar with the system they will prefer time-saving detailed and crowded pages to working through lots of simple choices.

Problems of writing for electronic text

One way of overcoming some of the difficulties presented by small grid configurations is to write text in smaller sections, to characterize such sections by headings, and to allow readers to pick and choose the sequences in which they will read the text by using a menu of section headings. In writing for a British electronic journal I have noted how I have been forced to use headings much more frequently so that readers can have this opportunity.

This procedure works reasonably well if the headings match readers' expectations or accepted practice. Scientific articles, for example, are (usually) clearly structured. There is usually an Abstract, Introduction, Method, Results, Discussion, Conclusion and Reference section – in that order. An electronic text presentation of such an article allows readers to select which bits they want to read in whatever order they choose. However, it might be more difficult to organize text which is less coherent.

Tabular and graphic material pose additional problems for electronic text. The nature of the system being used often means that graphics appear crude and amateurish, although some systems are better than others. None the less, even technically superior systems can have deficient graphics. Sometimes there are too many lines per graph, or three-dimensional presentations are used instead of simple bar charts. Comparisons between items (eg currencies) that have gone up or down relative to one another are difficult to grasp if they are presented in graphs that ascend and descend from a zero baseline.

Small screen configurations make it difficult to present complex tabular and graphic materials, especially if one wants to add captions and/or explanatory text. However, colour and animation are important considerations here and these will be discussed below.

The structure of tables in electronic text has to be as simple as possible and related to the way in which the tables are used. Because of the limits in size it is tempting to use abbreviations for row and column headings, but undoubtedly such procedures cause difficulties for readers. Once, when I was preparing an article for publication in an electronic journal, I decided that I had three options for dealing with a complex table. I could (a) divide it up into three separate tables, (b) simplify it – by excluding lots of detail, or (c) simplify it and let the reader know that more details were available in a series of tables in a later appendix. I chose option (b).

The point I am making here is that much material may have to be excluded from electronic text if small, low-resolution screens persist. Indeed, most of the illustrations used in this textbook could not appear today on the majority of screens if they were to be presented in electronic form. It seems surprising that few designers have discussed the possibility of integrating conventional and electronic text by, for example, providing workbooks to accompany computer-assisted instruction. Some practitioners (eg, British Gas and the Open University) have tried this successfully.

Compensating features

So far the discussion has proceeded as though electronic text had few redeeming features compared with print on paper. It is worth pointing out, therefore, that the main virtue of electronic text is that it does not use paper storage facilities, and that vast amounts of information can be stored in computer databases at (relatively) little cost.

With conventional text the paperwork can simply become too cumbersome. Duffy (1985) cites a study of a technical manual in which the investigators found that, in order to diagnose and repair one aircraft radar malfunction, a technician had to refer to 165 pages in eight documents and to look at 41 different places in these documents. One of the main benefits of electronic text is that it can accelerate access to such information. Systems can be devised which help the users to look for and to sift the information that they require. What is important about these systems is that what the readers see is much less than what they do not see.

Lancaster and Warner (1985) draw attention to Nelson's concept of 'hypertext'. This allows users to use the text in any way which is logical to them, rather than confining them to movement which is logical to the author. Specifically, Nelson talks of 'rapid jumps' – where material stored in one place may link with material stored in another place (possibly even in a different document). Such dynamic pathways through text are also part of Negroponte's system at Massachusetts Institute of Technology. Here the reader sits in a chair whose arms are fitted with a joystick and a touch-sensitive pad. These facilities, which include a zoom capability, are used to generate displays which fill up a whole wall with text or graphic information. Different sources can be brought together from different databases and displayed on adjacent screens.

Even more mundane electronic text, such as Ceefax or Prestel, has features not available with print-based text. These features, which will now be considered, may (or may not) compensate for some of the limitations of text design discussed earlier.

Signalling text

Various techniques can be used in electronic text to draw attention to particular words or parts of text. 'Flashing' and 'reverse-video' are two particular devices which may be used to call attention to particular items. Flashing occurs when a particular word or phrase appears brighter on the screen for short periods of time. Reverse-video allows part of the text to appear in dark on light rather than in the usual form of light on dark. In my view, flashing and reverse-video could easily be distracting features if they were over-used.

Presentation speed

With electronic text one does not need to present full 'screen-fulls' of text. Text can be separated and presented one line or one paragraph at a time and there is much debate concerning the advantages of different ways of *scrolling* text.

Scrolling can take several forms. The text may jump up, move up steadily, or even shift sideways. One line of text may be displayed at a time, or several lines of text may move up in chunks at a pace determined either automatically or by the reader. With some systems scrolling can be a property of different parts of the screen – thus some material may remain on screen while other material is scrolled. In other systems such scrolled parts may be magnified.

One might imagine that reading text which is moving up or down could cause the reader problems. Indeed, the limited research that there is on this topic does suggest that scrolling individual sentences one at a time can hinder recall, and that in general scrolling makes it more difficult to grasp the organization of a text. Kolers *et al* (1981) found that readers preferred smooth scrolling but that scrolling (at a subjectively pleasing rate) was less efficient than reading a static page. However, when scrolling was 20 per cent faster it produced more efficient reading than did the static page.

In an experiment on computer-assisted instruction (not involving scrolling), Bevan (1981) found that performance deteriorated when the speed of presentation was similar to or faster than the reading speeds of his adult participants. He recommended a speed of 10 to 15 characters per second when the task required learners to understand and retain material. He noted, however, that 10 characters per second may frustrate more able users, and that 15 characters per second might be a better choice, particularly when the material being studied has a high level of redundancy.

The use of colour

One of the most important features of electronic text is the availability of multi-coloured formats. In some systems many colours are used, but with Ceefax, Oracle and Prestel only seven colours are used (but each can form the background for the others). These seven are green, red, blue, magenta, cyan, yellow and white. In a comprehensive review of factors affecting the legibility of these seven colours, Reynolds (1980) suggests that green, white, yellow and cyan are the most useful colours to use on a dark background.

In the same way that italic or bold print might be used in conventional text, colour cueing can be used to emphasize particular words or phrases (eg red for DO NOT . . .). Colour can be used to indicate categories of importance – as in the News on Ceefax, where the main paragraphs appear in white and the subparagraphs in blue. Colour can be used in place of space to convey organization and structure. Thus rows or columns in tables (or groups of them) may be presented in alternating colours to aid retrieval. Studies show, however, that this can cause great difficulties if readers are expected to read both down and across the tables.

One particular problem with using colour cueing to convey text structure is that (unlike spatial cueing) there does not appear to be an intuitive range of colours that would suggest a hierarchy of importance. In addition, if colours are to be used in a meaningful way then the users must be able to distinguish between the functions of different colours and thus colour coding must not be excessive. Designers such as Reynolds (1980) suggest that the number of colours used on any one graph or chart should be kept to a minimum, that they should be used consistently, and that they should be clearly differentiated from other colours used in the wording of items on the screen.

Colour on colour.
An additional but related problem noted earlier is that it is of course possible to use different coloured backgrounds for electronic text (much as in the same way one can use different coloured paper in conventional printing). Galitz (1981) reports that the perception of sizes indicated by bar charts, for example, may depend upon the foreground and surrounding colours, and he cites a study which concluded that warm colours (red and yellow) usually appear larger than cooler colours (green and blue). Reynolds (1980) points out that when two colours are presented in close juxtaposition then the perception of each colour is modified by the other. Foster and Bruce (1982) recommend that when selecting colour on colour combinations, dark colours (red and blue) should be paired with light ones (white, yellow, cyan) and that neither two light nor two medium colours (green and magenta) should be used together.

Sound and graphics

Noisy animated graphics are compulsive features of video games and no doubt such features can be used to advantage in electronic text. A number of writers have pointed to the value of animation for showing cyclical changes – such as the operation of the internal combustion engine. Graphics can be used like film to show sequential processes and to build up understanding step by step. Unlike film, however, computer graphics can be run at various speeds under the control of the learner. Sound can be added to vision to provide reinforcement for success in instructional programmes for example.

In considering sound and animation for instruction, attention must be paid to their purpose – are they there for motivational or functional reasons (or both)? With graphics it is important not to overload the learner: animated graphics presented together with static text may provide too much information all at once. Hence it is important to evaluate the success of these devices.

Working with VDUs

At present there have been few studies which have examined the effects of doing lengthy tasks on a VDU and compared them with other methods (such as textbooks). One or two studies of children's reading suggest that they have no real difficulties with text displayed on a VDU if the text is at the appropriate difficulty level, but that when the text is difficult then readers slow down more with VDUs. Studies with adults using VDUs for long periods also suggest some slowing down with the VDU presentation.

Other evidence suggests that working uninterrupted for long periods of time with VDUs is likely to produce complaints of eyestrain, headaches and tiredness. It is, of course, difficult to know whether these complaints arise from working with VDUs – or from the fact that any job which requires individuals to remain in the same position, to focus on a fixed plane, and to concentrate for a long time without rest is likely to cause feelings of strain and tiredness. It is likely, however, that VDUs do contribute to these strains. No doubt many of the symptoms can be accounted for by inappropriate ergonomic factors – such as screen glare caused by too high a lighting level, inappropriate seating and working positions – as well as by ocular defects. None the less, poor legibility and inappropriate interline spacing may well lead to headaches (Wilkins, 1984). It would be agreeable to think that the strain of using VDUs could be reduced by using better designed instructional text.

Summary

1. **The legibility of electronic text is a function of many interacting variables in addition to those in printed text.**

2. **The findings from research on printed text suggest that the legibility of electronic text will be enhanced if the text is set unjustified and presented with consistent horizontal and vertical spacing to group and separate the relevant parts.**

3. **However, the presentation of electronic text is constrained at present by small grid configurations and limited graphics resolution. These produce problems both for readers and designers. Readers find it difficult to skim and find their way about such text. Designers find it difficult to present tabular and graphic materials.**

4. **The use of colour may help overcome some of these problems but there are a number of considerations that have to be born in mind if colour is to be used effectively.**

5. **The difficulties that readers experience when using VDUs for extended periods of time might be reduced by the use of better designed textual displays.**

Chapter 15

Evaluating instructional text

Instructional text can be evaluated in a number of different ways. This chapter discusses evaluation in terms of content, typography and teaching effectiveness. Case-histories are provided to indicate the value of the methods advocated in this textbook.

How can we evaluate instructional text? What questions must we ask and how can we answer them? A survey of the literature in this area reveals a concern with at least three main – but related – areas of enquiry. We can ask questions about a text's content, about its technical quality, and about its teaching effectiveness. Within each of these areas we can ask further questions about the methods available to help us make decisions about the value of a particular piece of instructional text.

How can one evaluate content?

Assessing the contents of instructional materials has been approached from many different points of view. In the field of textbook design there has been a concern with the accuracy, the suitability, and the difficulty of a text. When evaluating the contents of a text we look to see if there are outdated materials, if there are errors of facts or principles or unjustified inferences, and if there are biases of various kinds – nationalistic, racial and sexual. Instructional text, to be as useful as possible, must contain content that is accurate, unbiased, up-to-date, and sufficient for the purpose at hand.

This much seems obvious, but it is not obvious how to be sure that the content meets such qualifications. Not only are the above descriptions hard to specify but also at times they may be misleading. Users of technical documents sometimes complain, for instance, that such documents often contain *too much* information, that is, more than is needed for a task to be done. The same kind of problem can arise with textbooks. How much background information, of interest historically but now admittedly out of date or even inaccurate by current standards, should go into, say, a science textbook? And how can one be assured that bias is not present, except through rather subjective attempts to interpret today's shifting nationalistic, racial and sexual standards?

Evaluating content is, at best, a difficult activity for teachers or content experts. The most common way to increase objectivity and provide satisfactory coverage appears to be to use some sort of checklist. A report to Unesco from the Educational Products Information Exchange Institute entitled *Selecting Among Textbooks* contains – and critically comments on – a dozen examples of checklists which teachers can complete when assessing or making comparisons between textbooks. An extract from just one such checklist is provided in Figure 15/1.

It is important to note, of course, that the amount of freedom of choice given to teachers in selecting textbooks varies widely between different countries. In the 1959 Unesco report *Primary School Textbooks* it was reported that over 75 per cent of teachers in the USA had no say in the selection of textbooks, but the situation has changed somewhat today. Tulley and Farr (1985), for instance, report that the selection of textbooks is state-controlled in 22 states in the USA and delegated to school districts in 28 states. They further comment that the aim of state control is more to regulate publishers' practices than it is to exert pedagogic control. In other countries different procedures are used. In Norway, for instance, school texts are officially approved for a period of five years, and then they have to be re-examined to see if they can continue to be used.

Figure 15/1

A checklist for assessing textbooks.
(In the original version each item is
followed by a five-point rating scale
from very good to very bad.)

A. Format of book
1. General appearance
2. Practicality of size and colour for classroom use
3. Readability of type
4. Durability and flexibility of binding
5. Appeal of page layouts
6. Appropriateness of the illustrations
7. Usefulness of chapter headings
8. Usability of index
9. Quality of the paper

B. Organization and content
10. Consistency of the organization and emphases with the teaching and learning standards of the school
11. Consistency of the point of view of the book with the basic principles of the subject area for which the book is being considered
12. Usefulness in stimulating critical thinking
13. Aid in stimulating students forming their own goals and towards self-evaluation
14. Usefulness in providing situations for problem solving
15. Usefulness in furthering the systematic and sequential program of the course of study
16. Clarity and succinctness of the explanations
17. Interest appeal
18. Provision for measuring student achievement
19. Adequacy of the chapter organization
20. Adaptability of content to classroom situations and to varying abilities of individual students
21. Degree of challenge for the reasonably well-prepared students
22. Usefulness for the more able students
23. Usefulness for the slow learners
24. Adequacy of the quality and quantity of skills assignments
25. Provision for review and maintenance of skills previously taught

How can one evaluate technical quality?

Approximately half of the 70 countries surveyed in the Unesco (1959) report referred to the importance of the physical and typographic aspect of textbook production when evaluating textbooks. Many of these countries used sets of standards based on 'expert opinion' or 'official requirements'.

One of my aims in this textbook has been to question such standards, and yet, at the same time, to advocate some new ones. In advocating standards it is perhaps worthwhile to bear in mind the comments made in this respect by Buckingham (1931). Buckingham found that the standards advocated by Shaw in 1902 concerning line-length, size of print and interline space had become dogma for the next 20 years or so. Yet, as far as he could ascertain, these standards were 'apparently plucked out of the air'.

Buckingham also commented that the standards of 1902 had little relevance to the printing practices of his day (1931), and that the experimental tests of these standards had (because of the difficulty of experimentation in this area) obtained results of limited practical value. Buckingham's comments read as true today as when they were written – over 50 years ago. If it is still true that standards are mainly a result of traditional practice or 'common sense', that the printing methods of today are unlike those of 20 years ago, and that the research testing such standards is of limited value, then can anything of value be said about evaluating textbooks in these terms?

I have tried in this text to indicate how my approach to the design of instructional materials might help instructional effectiveness. To conclude this section of this chapter I have provided a summary checklist of the sorts of things (in terms of typographic decisions) that I would look for in evaluating a text typographically. I have framed each question so that an answer 'yes' indicates a positive response.

Checklist for the evaluation of typographic decision making in instructional materials

Organization of content
- ☐ Are the chapter divisions sufficiently clear?
- ☐ Are there summaries of the chapter content?
- ☐ Are heading levels coded clearly and consistently?
- ☐ Are subsections within the chapters clearly and consistently differentiated by the spatial organization of the text?
- ☐ Are there running headings at the top of each page?
- ☐ Is there an author and subject index?

Page detailing
- ☐ Has the material been printed on a standard page-size?
- ☐ Is the contents page clearly organized?
- ☐ Are the page numbers provided on the contents page easy to locate?
- ☐ If there are multiple tables, graphs, pictures, etc in the text, is a single-column format used?
- ☐ Is there consistent spacing between the words in each sentence?
- ☐ Are word-breaks at the ends of lines avoided?
- ☐ Is the vertical spacing consistent?
- ☐ Does the interrelationship between typesize, line-length, and interline space seem appropriate for the reader?
- ☐ Is the stopping point at the bottom of a page determined by the content?
- ☐ Are footnotes avoided?
- ☐ Will the typeface withstand repeated copying?
- ☐ Are the margins sufficient for binding, filing, etc?

The role of examples and illustrative material
- ☐ Does the illustrative material add to the text in any way?
- ☐ Is the illustrative material placed appropriately in the text, and in sequence within it?
- ☐ Does the illustrative material have clear captions?
- ☐ Are these captions positioned consistently throughout the text?
- ☐ If examples are provided in the text are these clearly recognizable as such?
- ☐ If tables, graphs, diagrams and examples are presented in the text are they clearly drawn so that retrieval from them is not difficult?
- ☐ If the text is mathematical are particular problems (eg equations) presented in a standard way throughout the text?
- ☐ Is the use of colour appropriate and consistent throughout the text?

How can one evaluate teaching effectiveness?

There are a variety of ways of assessing the teaching effectiveness of instructional text. In this chapter I shall first comment in more detail on the general notion of readability, and then consider the problems of making experimental comparisons.

Is readability related to teaching effectiveness?

We saw in Chaper 6 that one approach to assessing effectiveness of instructional texts is to examine them in terms of their readability or difficulty. One study in the United States, for example, assessed six series of elementary school science textbooks in these terms. It was found that books for younger children tended to be at an appropriate readability level but that books for older children varied more widely: indeed one of the texts studied varied in suitability for students between 14 and 20 years. Similar findings have been reported in the United Kingdom.

There are a number of different ways of assessing readability which, unfortunately, do not always yield the same results. As we saw in Chapter 6 the simplest procedures involve computing average word and sentence lengths and deriving appropriate age levels by applying certain formulas. Since such readability formulas are designed for use with prose text, problems arise with scientific, technical and mathematical material for these contain specialist vocabulary together with numerical and symbolic language. The difficulty to a child of $E = mc^2$ can hardly be assessed by a readability formula. Thus readability measures only measure a surface kind of readability and they take little account of the meaning of the text for the reader. (As we saw in Chapter 6 you would get the same result from a formula for a particular text even if the word order was reversed in every sentence.)

There have been several attempts to see whether or not teachers can match the difficulty of a text to a pupil's ability without using a readability formula. The results have shown that the ability to make such judgements varies widely between individuals. However, group measures (ie the average of the judgements of a set of teachers) seem to agree with measures derived from a single readability formula (Klare, 1976). It might be wiser, therefore, to use an appropriate readability formula than to rely on individual personal judgement to assess the difficulty level of various texts.

One particular point to note here is that textbook vocabulary which is considered normal for pupils in the USA or the UK is likely to be more difficult for pupils in developing countries. Indeed, there may be even greater variability in the reading abilities of pupils in such countries. Grade and age levels as determined by current American readability formulas may over-estimate the suitability of texts in these situations. So, in order to select a useful text one needs to know not only about readers' reading skills, but also about their background knowledge, and possibly their motivation. The more learners know about a topic, the more readable will be a text on that topic, and the easier they will find it. And, the more motivated learners are, the more they will persist. None the less, as we saw in Chapter 6, despite these difficulties the relative style difficulty of two texts with the same content area can be meaningfully compared with a readability formula. Many studies have shown advantages for more readable texts, particularly with less able readers.

Can the teaching effectiveness of instructional text be assessed by experiment?

Another area of research in textbook evaluation examines the way in which student performance is affected by features in the textbook used. There has been considerable research in this area with programmed textbooks, but remarkably little with conventional ones.

The research with programmed textbooks suggests three levels of approach which could also be applied to the evaluation of more conventional text. These are:

1. Evaluation of a text in comparison with some other teaching method (usually conventional instruction);

2. Evaluation of the success of a text in achieving its overall objectives; and

3. Manipulation of variables within a text in order to see what effect this has on student performance.

Comparison studies.
Considerable research has been undertaken comparing programmed textbooks with instruction by some other method (usually classroom instruction). Tests of knowledge are usually administered before and after the instruction, and sometimes also at a later date to assess long-term retention. The general picture provided by such studies indicates (i) that programmed texts can often teach as well as teachers can (and sometimes better); (ii) that usually they can do this in the same amount of time (and sometimes faster); and (iii) that programmed texts and teachers working together produce better results than either working separately. I can trace no reports, however, of this sort of experimental approach with conventional textbooks, although there are studies which show that increasing the availability of textbooks in less-developed countries leads to better (tested) performance.

Some investigators have argued that countries which have centralized systems of textbook selection could carry out research of this kind with conventional textbooks. Comparisons could be made between different textbooks on the same topic and comparisons could be made between original and redesigned versions of textbooks – comparisons in terms of costs of production as well as teaching effectiveness.

Achieving objectives.
We saw in Chapter 8 that a standard procedure in the construction of a programmed text involves a careful test-revise-test-again sequence. The aim of this is to see how well the stated aims of the text are being achieved and to revise the text in the light of the results obtained. And, as we noted in Chapter 12, similar procedures are being used in form design.

In some countries this procedure has been adopted for developing conventional textbooks – the Unesco (1959) survey reported that experimental versions of textbooks were published and tested in about 10 per cent of the countries studied. And at a recent conference in New Zealand six out of eight developing countries reported field testing in this way. In other countries less formal procedures are used during the writing of textbooks. Colleagues and experts are asked to read and advise, but children – for whom the material is intended – are not often involved in pre-publication testing.

None the less, such a user-oriented process is now beginning to be used more widely by authors of instructional text. Pat Wright (1979) for instance argues that instructional text can be subjected to 'quality control': text can be evaluated in terms of its content, presentation and usability. She suggests that different evaluation techniques are appropriate for these different areas, thus: *Content* can be evaluated by field studies, interviews, and surveys; *Presentation* can be evaluated by field studies, surveys, and laboratory experiments; *Usability* can be evaluated by interviews and laboratory experiments.

To all of these techniques she adds one more: the 'critical appraisal' of experts in all three areas. Wright discusses the advantages and limitations of all these different methods for evaluating instructional text. She points out (i) that there is no one perfect method, and (ii) that it is helpful to use more than one method of evaluation.

Manipulating variables within texts.
A third feature of research with programmed texts has been the systematic manipulation of variables within the text in order to assess their effectiveness. Thus in programmed learning there have been experiments on step-sizes, on active versus passive responding, and on different ways of providing knowledge of results for the learner, just to list three sets of variables. There has been some attempt to do this kind of research with more conventional text: several experiments have been done comparing different ways of presenting text. Much of this work, however, has been limited and often it has taken place with short documents rather than complete texts.

Some difficulties in doing experimental studies

It is this last sort of approach that I have been most interested in in my own research. I believe that research in this field will only advance when typographers and psychologists work together to derive generalizable solutions to a set of real-life practical problems. This means starting off with specific problems, arriving at a variety of solutions, selecting the ones that seem most possible, and then evaluating their success. The evaluation will be limited because (i) it is not possible to evaluate and compare every possible solution to a problem, (ii) the methods which we have at our disposal for evaluation in this area tend to be somewhat limited, and (iii) different measures have their own in-built assumptions. (Most techniques, for example, seem to assume that the reader starts at the beginning of a text and reads through it steadily to the end.)

None the less I believe it is important to conduct evaluation studies for two main reasons. First of all, it is easy to assume that because you have redesigned something, there must be an improvement. Such suppositions need to be tested. For example, I once spent four days re-organizing a piece of instructional text, and I was sure that my students would much prefer the revised version. However, when I asked them, 10 out of 20 students preferred the original. Similarly, I once resequenced the position of some illustrations in a technical article so that each one came into line with its textual reference. I did not think that this would make a great deal of difference to how people would judge the effectiveness of the text but, to my surprise, 19 out of 20 students preferred the resequenced passage. So the first point is that psychologists, designers and typographers all need to test their intuitions against reality.

The second reason for evaluating one's decision making lies with making advances in scientific knowledge. If something works, then we can begin to find out more about how and why this is so. We can begin to refine our experimentation. At the moment, it is probably true to say that opening up text by using a system of proportional spacing and making the text more readable will aid the comprehension of a complex text. But so will other methods – as argued by other authors in other textbooks. So what are the critical parameters? And how do they combine? Evaluation will help us to decide.

What measures are available?

Evaluating decisions, of course, presents the researcher with methodological difficulties and with problems of measurement. Over the last ten years or so my colleagues and I have used a variety of measures (and combinations of them) to test our ideas. Table 15/1 tries to encapsulate some of the strengths and limitations of these measures. I have divided them into five main groups. Opposite these five blocks are my estimates of the reliability of these measures and some comments about them. Inspection of the table shows that some measures are more reliable than others, and common sense indicates that some measures are more suitable than others for different purposes. Thus oral reading measures give detailed information about specific reading difficulties; search and retrieval tasks are appropriate for evaluating the layout of highly structured text; comprehension measures are more appropriate for evaluating the effectiveness of continuous prose; and readability and preference measures are useful as additional sources of information.

A different kind of measure, not listed in Table 15/1, is that of the *cost* to produce various solutions to a design problem. As I have noted earlier, considerable cost savings can be gained by the use of unjustified settings, narrower margins, thinner paper, and modern printing methods. In our experiments we have sometimes shown reductions in cost without any loss of comprehension and sometimes great improvement in comprehension for a slight increase in cost (see below). Results such as these point in particular to the hidden costs of poor quality materials.

Table 15/1 Methods used in typographic research, and their reliability.

Method	Estimated reliability	Test-retest correlations obtained in our studies	Comments
Reading aloud	High	0.78 to 0.95	Insensitive to differences in layouts
Reading aloud (text upside down)	Very high	0.87 to 0.99	Slows reading right down; larger spreads of scores with males than females
Scanning technical material	High	0.75 to 0.91	Good for technical materials: sensitive
Scanning prose[1] (short intervals)	Moderate	0.49 to 0.68	Moderately useful and sensitive
Scanning prose[1] (wide intervals)	Low	0.36 to 0.83	Poor: searchers 'get lost'
Silent reading speed (without test)	Fairly high	0.53 to 0.96	The researcher does not know what has been read
Silent reading speed (with test to follow)	Fairly high	0.70 to 0.82	Knowledge of forthcoming test slows readers down markedly
Comprehension (cloze test)[2]	Fairly high	0.55 to 0.95	Useful for assessing relative difficulty
Comprehension (recall questions)	Low	0.46 to 0.73	Too specific to make comparisons with, if different materials are used
Preferences	Fairly high	0.72	Useful as an additional measure
Readability formulas	Very high	(not applicable)	Useful as an additional measure

[1] Scanning involves providing the reader with a list of phrases drawn from the text, each with a word missing. The reader has to scan (or skim) the text, find the phrase, and write in the missing word.

[2] The cloze test involves providing the reader with a text with, say, every seventh word missing. The reader has to supply the missing words.

Case-histories

Finally, to complete this chapter, I shall present six case-histories of evaluation studies. Taken together, these studies indicate that there are sometimes financial and sometimes instructional gains to be achieved by following the guidelines presented in this text.

Case-history 1. The prospectus study

In Chapter 2 I described how a reference grid was essential to the design of highly structured text, and I used as an example two pages from a college prospectus (see Figure 2/1d). In fact the whole prospectus was redesigned along the lines outlined in Chapters 1 to 4. This revised prospectus was evaluated in two ways: (i) by looking at how students used the prospectus, and (ii) by examining production costs.

The full details of this study have been presented elsewhere (Burnhill *et al*, 1975). What we need to note here is that when using search and retrieval tasks with the college students, we were unable to find any differences between their ability to use the original and the revised prospectus. What was obvious was the great range of times taken to find anything in both versions! However, in terms of costs we were able to produce the revised prospectus (which was slightly larger) at a cheaper rate – at a time of rapid inflation. The cost of the original prospectus for £1,470 for 8,000 copies. (This excluded charges for author's corrections which, in fact, amounted to several hundred pounds.) The cost of the revised prospectus a year later was £1,180 for 7,500 copies. (There were no charges for author's corrections for these were set off against errors made by the printer with respect to the specification.) In this example, therefore, the revised prospectus was as effective as the original prospectus, and this was achieved at a greatly reduced cost.

Case-history 2. A complex legal document

In Chapter 5 examples 5a and 5b show part of the original and part of a redesigned version of a leaflet distributed by the British Psychological Society. To test the efficiency of the redesign both versions were typed on A4 paper, and then reduced to A5 (thus simulating printed text). The original document covered four A5 pages, and the revised version five A5 pages.

Groups of undergraduate students were asked to carry out a number of search tasks using the two documents. The results (described in detail by Hartley and Burnhill, 1976) were quite conclusive. With the original layout six out of 23 students (26 per cent) were able to find all the items of business to be discussed at the meeting: with the revised version 18 out of 21 (86 per cent) found them. With the original layout only 12 out of 23 students (48 per cent) were able to find the four special resolutions which were to be discussed, whereas with the revised version 20 out of 21 (95 per cent) found them. The times taken to retrieve these items were significantly faster for students using the revised version.

In this example then, in terms of paper costs, the revised edition of the pamphlet was more expensive. In terms of cost-effectiveness, however, the revised edition was clearly superior. As this document (like Figure 5/4a) was concerned with subscription matters, it would seem wise to opt for effective communication than to skimp on presentation.

Case-history 3. Tables in text

In the two case-histories above I have described the evaluation of a total product – a prospectus or a leaflet – and I have compared traditional printing practices with a more modern approach. In this third case-history I am concerned with examining variations within a range of possible solutions to a problem, all of which might be printed in a similar way.

In this study, which has been described in detail elsewhere (Burnhill *et al*, 1976), we inserted tables of information into a four-page article printed on A4 paper. The text was printed in a two-column or a single-column format, and the tables cut across the two-column format. Approximately 340 schoolchildren, aged between 12 and 14 and of a wide ability range, searched the text (using the method of scanning). The results showed that there was a clear effect due to the presence of single or double columns. The children did significantly better with the single-column format, and this result was repeated whether or not they were of high or low ability.

The findings of this study suggest, therefore, that a single-column structure for the text on an A4 page may be preferable to a double-column one for complex text containing various components. These findings reinforce the view that decisions concerning the column structure of a page should not be decided on by a simple concern for line-length but should also take into account the structural requirements of the text and its non-textual components.

Case-history 4. Readability

Consider the following passage:

> The rapidly growing wealth of Britain during the reign of the first four Georges not only brought increased comfort; it also helped to inspire a great achievement in the arts. Later, under Queen Victoria, wealth became widely spread among people who had no family background of culture and little artistic taste, and were therefore liable either to ignore art altogether or to spend money on buildings and pictures of little merit. In the eighteenth century, wealth was still piling up in the hands of the landed aristocracy, who with their great houses and their 'Grand Tours' abroad had by now a traditional interest in art. These noblemen established admirable standards of taste in painting and architecture which others were generally content to follow. And in literature, where authors came to depend as the century progressed not on the patronage of an individual nobleman but on the favour of a small, cultured upper and upper-middle class, the achievement was no less brilliant.

This passage was found in an old history textbook available for 12- to 13-year-old children to read. The passage has a Flesch reading grade level of 14.5 which suggests that it is more suitable for 19-year-olds than for the 12- to 13-year-olds who were reading it!

To revise this passage one of my undergraduate students, Christine Williams, carried out the following procedures:

1. She shortened the sentences: for example, long complex sentences were turned into two simpler ones.

2. She replaced unusual words by more common ones: for example, 'established' became 'set up'.

3. She replaced metaphorical phrases by literal ones: for example, 'under Queen Victoria' became 'in Queen Victoria's reign'.

4. She added phrases which made the digression in time clearer to the reader.

This led to the following passage:

> The wealth of Britain grew quickly in the eighteenth century, during the reigns of the first four King Georges. This caused better living conditions for people in Britain. It also helped to bring about some fine achievements in designing buildings, in paintings and in other arts. Later, in Queen Victoria's reign, wealth became more widespread among ordinary people, who did not come from families which had been interested in the arts for many years. These people were likely either to ignore the arts or to spend money on buildings and paintings of low standard. In the previous eighteenth century it was those born in the already rich land owning families who had become wealthier. These noblemen, with their grand houses and tours abroad, had a traditional family interest in the arts. They set up high standards of taste in painting and building design which other people followed. As time went by in the eighteenth century the writers of books and poetry also achieved high standards. The reasons for this were not only that the noblemen were interested in their work but also that men from the upper and middle classes took an interest.

This version has a Flesch reading grade level of 11 which suggests that it is now suitable for 15-year-olds.

To assess the effectiveness of this version children in two classes of 12- to 13-year-olds (one of high and one of middle ability) were given one or other of the two versions of the passage. They were asked first to read their passage for a period of ten minutes, and then to write down as if for an absent friend the main points of the passage. Independent judges scored these recalls. Making the passage more readable did not have any effect with the able children (Class 1) but it significantly helped the less able ones (Class 2).

The findings of such a case-history are typical of several studies of this kind (see Hartley, 1981, for references). It should be noted, however, that some researchers recommend that readability formulas should *not* be used to evaluate or develop texts. The main objection being that it is unwise to use a formula for rewriting text. The argument is that if one just simplifies text by splitting sentences, removing connectives, and simplifying the odd multi-syllabic word, then the resulting text is likely to be stilted, lacking in clear organization and, in fact, harder to understand.

Case-history 5. Using multiple measures

Figures 7/2a and 7/2b in Chapter 7 illustrate an original and a revised version of a page from a technical document. To compare the effectiveness of these revisions to the total document (three pages long) five different measures were used. The purpose of this case-history is to show how different measures might produce different results, but how a combination of measures leads to a broader overall picture. The results were as follows:

- In terms of *readability* the first 100 words of the original document (excluding headings) had a reading age level of 19.5 years, whereas the first 100 words of the revised version had a reading age level of 15 years (Gunning FOG index).
- In terms of *reading speed* there were no significant differences between the average times taken by two groups of ten university students to read the three pages set in either version.
- In terms of *factual recall*, however, these same groups of students recalled an average of 5.4 out of 10 for the original and 7.9 out of 10 for the revised version. (This difference is statistically significant.)
- In terms of *preferences*, seven out of ten of my colleagues chose the revised version in preference to the original when asked to judge which figure they found 'the clearer'. (This difference, while pleasing, is not statistically significant.)
- When reading speed and factual recall measures were repeated in a *replication* study with a further 20 students, the results were almost exactly repeated.

This composite picture allowed me to suggest that the revised version was easier to read, that the students extracted more information per unit time, and that judges were more likely to prefer the revised version.

Case-history 6. Extended studies

This case-history is introduced to suggest that in order to assess the effectiveness of one (or more) particular variables in text design, it is necessary to run a series of experiments with built-in replications and extensions. Thus, for example, in a series of 17 studies my colleagues and I have assessed the effectiveness of inserting headings in instructional text. These studies have involved multiple-measurements, different passages, and built-in replications. A summary of some of the findings is as follows:

- Four out of four studies indicated that headings significantly reduced the time taken to find information in unfamiliar text;
- Four out of four studies indicated that headings significantly reduced the time taken to retrieve familiar information from a passage;
- Three out of five studies indicated that headings significantly aided factual recall (immediately after reading the passage);
- None out of six studies indicated that the form of headings (questions or statements) had any significant effect upon search, retrieval or recall;
- None out of nine studies indicated that the position of headings (marginal or embedded) had any significant effect upon search, retrieval or recall.

As noted above this approach of steadily extending one's field of enquiry with built-in replication studies is possibly the only way there is to evaluate the effects of one particular variable in text. Even here (as in Dwyer's case discussed in Chapter 9) the findings are limited to the materials used, the questions asked, and to the age and ability levels of the participants involved.

Concluding comments on the case-histories

Experimental methods of assessing text are limited. It is rare to assess complete texts, and studies have many limitations. None the less, I maintain that testing in a limited way is better than not testing at all – for the reasons given earlier. The results provide us with information which accumulates and which we may (or may not) be able to capitalize on in subsequent decision making.

Summary

1. The contents of instructional materials can be checked for accuracy, bias, etc by using rating scales and questionnaires.

2. The technical quality of a text can be assessed with the checklist provided.

3. The difficulty level of materials can be checked using a readability formula.

4. Different methods of evaluation suit different objectives. A combination of measures is likely to be more useful than one measure alone.

5. The case-histories presented in this chapter suggest that the methods of text design advocated in this textbook can lead to gains in instructional effectiveness and/or gains in cost savings.

Appendix

An annotated bibliography

This bibliography is divided into six sections. Section 1 lists generally useful reference works. Section 2 provides references relevant to each of the preceding chapters. Section 3 lists resource materials in the form of journals. Section 4 gives titles from relevant British and American Standards. Sections 5 and 6 list the names and addresses of relevant centres of research in the United Kingdom and North America.

Section 1.   General reference works

The following texts contain broad overview research summaries of much of the material discussed in this textbook.

Duffy, T. & Waller, R. (Eds) (1985)
Designing Usable Texts.
Orlando, Florida: Academic Press.

Easterby, R. & Zwaga, H. (Eds) (1984)
Information Design.
Chichester: Wiley.

Jonassen, D.H. (Ed) (1982)
The Technology of Text Vol. 1.
Englewood Cliffs, NJ: Educational Technology Publications.

Jonassen, D.H. (Ed) (1985)
The Technology of Text Vol. 2.
Englewood Cliffs, NJ: Educational Technology Publications.

Kolers, P.A., Wrolstad, M.E. & Bouma, H. (Eds) (1979)
Processing of Visible Language Vol. 1.
New York: Plenum.

Kolers, P.A., Wrolstad, M.E. & Bouma, H. (Eds) (1980)
Processing of Visible Language Vol. 2.
New York: Plenum.

Section 2.   Further reading related to the chapters in this book

Chapters 1 and 2   A rational approach to typographic planning is discussed in a number of papers. Some of the most accessible are as follows:

Crouwel, W. (1979)
Typography: a technique of making text legible.
In P.A. Kolers *et al* (Eds) *Processing of Visible Language Vol. 1*.
New York: Plenum.

Goldring, M. (1967)
Rational typographic design.
In W. Jaspert (Ed) *Advances in Computer Typesetting*.
London: Institute of Printing.

Goldring, M. (1984)
Has the revolution in the composition of type improved typography?
Information Design Journal, 4, 1, 77-82.

Goldring, M. & Hackelsberger, A. (1973)
A standard specification for print production.
The Penrose Annual.

Chapters 3 and 4   The books referred to in these chapters are as follows:

Tinker, M.A. (1963)
Legibility of Print.
Ames: Iowa State University Press.

The Washburn College Bible (1980)
New York: Oxford University Press.

Watts, L. & Nisbet, J. (1974)
Legibility in Children's Books.
London: National Foundation for Educational Research.

Zachrisson, B. (1965)
Legibility of Printed Text.
Stockholm: Almqvist & Wiksell.

Research on unjustified and 'chunked' text is summarized by:

Hartley, J. (1981)
Eighty ways of improving instructional text.
IEEE Transactions on Professional Communication, PC-24, 1, 17-27.

Keenan, S.A. (1984)
Effects of chunking and line length on reading efficiency.
Visible Language, XVIII, 1, 61-80.

Two texts which illustrate the variety of typefaces and typesizes available are:

Jaspert, W.P., Berry, W.T. & Johnson, A.F. (1970)
The Encyclopaedia of Typefaces (Fourth Edition).
London: Blandford.

King, J.C. & Esposito, T. (1980)
Designer's Guide to Type.
New York: Van Nostrand Reinhold.

A study of the effects of the degradation of print caused by repeated copying is that of:

Spencer, H., Reynolds, L. & Coe, B. (1977)
The effects of image degradation and background noise on the legibility of text and numerals in four different typefaces.
Readability of Print Research Unit. London: Royal College of Art.

Chapter 5   The reference for Ian Dennis's paper (Example 6) is:

Dennis, I. (1975)
The design and experimental testing of a hospital drug labelling system.
Programmed Learning & Educational Technology, 12, 2, 88-94.

The general textbooks referred to in Section 1 of this bibliography present other 'before and after' examples.

Appendix

A text illustrating alternative layouts for university material is:

Macdonald-Ross, M. & Waller, R. (1975)
Open University Texts: Criticisms and Alternatives.
Institution of Educational Technology, Open University.

Chapter 6   The guidelines discussed in this chapter are largely based upon the following review of the research literature:

Hartley, J. (1981)
Eighty ways of improving instructional text.
IEEE Transactions on Professional Communication, PC-24, 1, 17-27.

The specific articles mentioned are as follows:

Chapanis, A. (1965)
Words, words, words.
Human Factors 7, 1, 1-17.

Felker, D.B. (Ed) (1980)
Document Design: A Review of Research.
Report available from the Document Design Center, American Institutes for Research, 1055 Thomas Jefferson Street, NW, Washington, DC 20007.

Hartley, J. (1984)
The role of colleagues and text-editing programs in improving text.
IEEE Transactions on Professional Communication, PC-27, 1, 42-44.

Johnstone, H. & Cassels, J. (1978)
What's in a word?
New Scientist, 73, 1103, 432-434.

Posner, G.J. & Strike, K.A. (1978)
Principles of sequencing content.
In J. Hartley & I.K. Davies (Eds) *Contributions to an Educational Technology Vol. 2.* London: Kogan Page/New York: Nichols.

There are several general texts on writing. A selection is as follows:

Mosenthal, P., Tamor, L. & Walmsley, S.A. (Eds) (1983)
Research on Writing.
New York: Longmans.

Murray, D. (1984)
Write to Learn.
New York: Holt, Rinehart & Winston.

Smith, F. (1982)
Writing and the Writer.
London: Heinemann.

The journals *Plain English, Simply Stated* and *Transactions on Professional Communication* contain many practical articles and *Written Communication* is a useful source of more theoretical ideas (see Section 3 of this bibliography).

The number of textbooks on computer-aided writing has increased dramatically since the mid-1980s. Two recent texts are:

Beach, R. & Bridwell, L. (Eds) (1984)
New Directions in Composition Research.
New York: Guildford Press.

Wresch, W. (Ed) (1984)
A Writer's Tool: The Computer in Composition Instruction.
Urbana: NCTE (1111 Kenyon Road, Urbana, Illinois 61801).

Chapter 8   The specific references mentioned in this chapter are:

Biran, L.A. (1967)
A comparison of a 'scrambled' and a 'sequential' presentation of a branching program.
Programmed Learning & Educational Technology, 4, 4, 290-295.

Horn, R.E. (1976)
How to Write Information Mapping.
Information Mapping Inc, 235 Wyman Street, Waltham, MA 02154, USA.

Horn, R.E. (1985)
Results with structured writing using the Information Mapping writing service standards.
In T. Duffy and R. Waller (Eds) *Designing Usable Texts.*
Orlando, Florida: Academic Press.

Krohn, G.S. (1983)
Flow charts used for procedural instructions.
Human Factors, 25, 5, 573-581.

Motil, J. (1984)
Programming Principles: An Introduction.
Boston: Allyn and Bacon.

Steinberg, E. (1984)
Teaching Computers to Teach.
Hillsdale, NJ: Erlbaum.

Wright, P. & Reid, F. (1973)
Written information: some alternatives to prose for expressing the outcomes of complex contingencies.
Journal of Applied Psychology, 57, 2, 160-166.

Further books and articles of interest are as follows:

Fields, A. (1983)
Information mapping: an overall appraisal.
Programmed Learning & Educational Technology, 20, 4, 276-282.

Megarry, J., Walker, D.R.F., Nisbet, J. & Hoyle, E. (Eds) (1983)
The World Yearbook of Education 1982/83: Computers and Education.
London: Kogan Page/New York: Nichols.

Richards, C. & Johnson, R. (1980)
Graphic codes for flow-charts.
Information Design Journal, 1, 4, 261-270.

Chapter 9   The specific references mentioned in this chapter are:

Bogusch, B.B. (1983)
Effects of five different picture placements in printed text on the acquisition
and retention of verbal information and concrete concepts.
Unpublished PhD thesis, College of Education, Florida State University.

Booher, H.R. (1975)
Relative comprehensibility of pictorial information and printed words in
proceduralized instructions.
Human Factors, 17, 3, 266-277.

Brody, P.J. (1982)
Affecting instructional textbooks through pictures.
In D. Jonassen (Ed) *The Technology of Text Vol. 1*.
Englewood Cliffs, NJ: Educational Technology Publications.

Dwyer, F.M. (1972)
A Guide for Improving Visualized Instruction.
Learning Services, Box 784, State College, Pennsylvania 16801.

Dwyer, F.M. (1976)
Adapting media attributes for effective learning.
Educational Technology, August, 7-13.

Dwyer, F.M. (1978)
Strategies for Improving Visual Learning.
Learning Services, Box 784, State College, Pennsylvania 16801.

Holliday, W. (1973)
Critical analysis of pictorial research related to science teaching.
Science Education, 57, 2, 201-214.

Levie, W.H. & Lentz, R. (1982)
Effects of text illustrations: a review of research.
Educational Communication and Technology Journal, 30, 4 195-232.

Murphy, C.M. & Wood, D.J. (1981)
Learning from pictures: the use of pictorial information by young children.
Journal of Experimental and Child Psychology, 32, 279-297.

Szlichcinski, C. (1984)
Factors affecting the comprehension of pictographic instruction.
In R. Easterby and H. Zwaga (Eds) *Information Design*.
Chichester: Wiley.

Twyman, M. (1979)
A schema for the study of graphic language.
In P.A. Kolers *et al* (Eds) *Processing of Visual Language Vol. 1*.
New York: Plenum.

Waller, R., Lefrere, P. & Macdonald-Ross, M. (1982)
Do you need that second color?
IEEE Transactions on Professional Communication, PC-25, 2 80-85.

Zimmerman, M.L. & Perkin, G.W. (1982)
Instructing people through pictures: print materials for people who do not read.
Information Design Journal, 3, 2, 119-134.

The review by Levie and Lentz (cited above) also contains references to studies of the role of pictures in learning to read; the effects of drawing one's own illustrations on comprehension; and learning to read maps.

Further books and articles of interest are as follows:

Harrison, R.P. (1981)
The Cartoon: Communication to the Quick.
Beverly Hills: Sage.

Lamberski, R.J. & Dwyer, F.M. (1983)
The instructional effect of coding (colour and black and white) on information acquisition and retrieval.
Educational Communication and Technology Journal, 31, 1, 9-22.

Schorr, F. (1984)
The effects of varying procedural instructions on comprehension.
Paper available from the author, Cornell University, Stone Hall, Ithaca, NY 14853.

Seddon, G.M. *et al* (1984)
The responsiveness of students to pictorial depth cues and the understanding of diagrams of three-dimensional structures.
British Educational Research Journal, 10, 1, 49-62.

Sewell, E.H. & Moore, R.L. (1980)
Cartoon embellishments in informative presentations.
Educational Communication and Technology Journal, 28, 1, 39-46.

Sless, D. (1981)
Learning and Visual Communication.
London: Croom Helm.

Chapter 10   The specific references mentioned in this text are:

Bartram, D. (1984)
The presentation of information about bus services.
In R. Easterby & H. Zwaga (Eds) *Information Design.*
Chichester: Wiley.

Ehrenberg, A.S.C. (1977)
Rudiments of numeracy.
Journal of the Royal Statistical Society A, 140, 227-297.

Macdonald-Ross, M. (1977)
Graphics in text.
In L.S. Shulman (Ed) *Review of Research in Education Vol. 5.*
Itasca, Illinois: Peacock.

Macdonald-Ross, M. (1977)
How numbers are shown: a review of research on the presentation of
quantitative data in texts.
Audio Visual Communication Review, 25, 359-409.

Tufte, E.R. (1983)
The Visual Display of Quantitative Information.
Graphics Press, Box 430, Cheshire, Connecticut 06410.

Wright, P. (1980)
The comprehension of tabulated information: some similarities between
reading prose and reading tables.
NSPI Journal, XIX, 8, 25-29.

Further articles of interest are as follows:

Milroy, R. & Poulton, E.C. (1979)
Labelling graphs for improved reading speed.
IEEE Transactions on Professional Communication, PC-22, 1, 30-33.

Wainer, H. (1980)
A test of graphicacy in children.
Applied Psychological Measurement, 4, 3, 331-340.

A useful discussion (and a rather different approach) is provided by:

Jones, B.F. *et al* (1984)
Considerate graphic texts.
Chapter 6 in *Content-Driven Comprehension, Instruction and Assessment: A
Model for Army Training Literature.*
Technical Report, Alexandria, VA: Army Research Institute.

Chapter 11   The specific references mentioned in this chapter are:

Curran, T.E. (1978)
Quantification of technical manual graphic comprehensibility.
Report TN-78-2, Navy Personnel Research and Development Center,
San Diego, California 92152.

Jones, B.F. *et al* (1984)
Considerate graphic texts.
Chapter 6 in *Content-Driven Comprehension, Instruction and Assessment: A
Model for Army Training Literature.*
Technical Report, Alexandria, VA: Army Research Institute.

Macdonald-Ross, M. (1977)
How numbers are shown: a review of research on the presentation of
quantitative data in texts.
Audio Visual Communication Review, 25, 359-409.

Tufte, E.R. (1983)
The Visual Display of Quantitative Information.
Graphics Press, Box 430, Cheshire, Connecticut 06410.

Zwaga, H. & Easterby, R. (1984)
Developing effective symbols for public information.
In R. Easterby & H. Zwaga (Eds) *Information Design*.
Chichester: Wiley.

Further items of interest are:

Kinross, R. (1981)
On the influence of Isotype.
Information Design Journal, 2, 2, 122-130.

Malter, M. (1947)
The ability of children to read cross-sections.
Journal of Educational Psychology, 38, 157-166.

Malter, M. (1947)
The ability of children to read a process diagram.
Journal of Educational Psychology, 38, 290-298.

Neurath, O. (1936)
International Picture Language.
(Re-issued 1980, Department of Typography and Graphic Communication, University of Reading, UK.)

Chapter 12   The specific references mentioned in this chapter are:

Felker, D.B. & Rose, A.M. (1981)
The Evaluation of a Public Document.
Technical Report No. 11, Document Design Center, American Institutes for Research, Washington, DC.

Firth, D. (1981)
An investigation of the success of re-designed supplementary benefit documents.
Information Design Journal, 2, 1, 33-43.

Lefrere, P. *et al* (1983)
Effective Forms.
Report available from The Institute of Educational Technology, The Open University, Milton Keynes MK7 6AA.

Mullarky, W. (1976)
(A report describing this research can be found in *Modern Office Procedures*, November, 1977.)

Rucker, M.H. & Arbaugh, J.E. (1979)
A comparison of matrix questionnaires with standard questionnaires.
Educational and Psychological Measurement, 39, 3, 637-643.

Waller, R. (1984)
Designing a government form: a case study.
Information Design Journal, 4, 36-57.

Wright, P. (1981/84)
Informed design for forms.
Either in *Information Design Journal* 1981, *2*, 151–178
or in R. Easterby and H. Zwaga (Eds) *Information Design*.
Chichester: Wiley.

Further useful books and guides on form design are:

Burgess, J. (1984)
Human Factors in Forms Design.
Chicago: Nelson.

Department of Health and Social Security (1983)
The Good Forms Guide.
London: DHSS Forms Unit (Ray House, 6 St Andrews Street, London EC4 3AD).

Felker, D.B. *et al* (1981)
Guidelines for Document Designers.
Document Design Center, American Institutes for Research, Washington, DC.

A special issue of *Information Design Journal* (Vol. 2, parts 3 and 4, 1981) is devoted to form design.

Chapter 13   The specific references on contents pages mentioned in this chapter are:

Hartley, J. (1980)
Designing journal contents pages: the role of spatial and typographic cues.
Journal of Research Communication Studies, 2, 83-98.

Hartley, J. & Guile, C. (1981)
Designing journal contents pages: preferences for horizontal and vertical layouts.
Journal of Research Communication Studies, 2, 271-288.

The references on references are:

Hartley, J. (1981)
Sequencing the elements in references: a reply to Shackel.
Applied Ergonomics, 12, 1, 7-12.

Hartley, J., Trueman, M. & Burnhill, P. (1979)
The role of spatial and typographic cues in the layout of journal references.
Applied Ergonomics, 10, 3, 165-169.

The references on bibliographies are:

Reynolds, L. (1979)
Visual Presentation of Information in Library Catalogues: A Survey.
Vol. 1 *Text*, Vol. 2 *Appendices*.
British Library Research and Development Report No. 5472.
London: British Library.

Reynolds, L. & Spencer, H. (1979)
Two experiments in the layout of computer output microfilm.
Graphic Information Research Unit. London: Royal College of Art.

Spencer, H. & Reynolds, L. (1976)
Factors affecting the acceptability of microforms as a reading medium.
Readability of Print Research Unit. London: Royal College of Art.

Spencer, H., Reynolds, L. & Coe, B. (1974)
Typographic coding in lists and bibliographies.
Applied Ergonomics, 5, 3, 136-141.

Spencer, H., Reynolds, L. & Coe, B. (1975)
Spatial and typographic cueing with bibliographical entries.
Programmed Learning & Educational Technology, 12, 2, 95-101.

The references on indexes are:

Bowman, S. *et al* (1983)
(reported in *Simply Stated*, No. 44, March, 1984)

Burnhill, P., Hartley, J. & Davies, L. (1977)
Typographic decision-making: the layout of indexes.
Applied Ergonomics, 8, 1, 35-39.

Dillon, M. & MacDonald, L.K. (1983)
Fully automatic book indexing.
Journal of Documentation, 39, 3, 135-154.

Gordon, C. (1983)
Teaching the young to use indexes.
The Indexer, 13, 3, 181-182.

Hartley, J., Davies, L. & Burnhill, P. (1981)
Alphabetization in indexes: experimental studies.
The Indexer, 12, 3, 149-153.

Jones, K.P. (1983)
How do we index: a report of some Aslib Informatics Group activity.
Journal of Documentation, 39, 1, 1-23.

Keen, E.M. (1976)
A retrieval comparison of six published indexes in the field of library and information science.
Unesco Bulletin for Libraries, 30, 1, 26-36.

Articles of further interest are:

Bryant, P. (1984)
Reading library catalogues and indexes.
Visible Language XVIII, 2, 142-153.
(NB: Figure captions are incorrectly positioned.)

Crystal, D. (1984)
Linguistics and indexing.
The Indexer, 14, 1, 3-7.

The Indexer usually contains lively debates on all matters concerning indexing.

Appendix

Chapter 14   The specific references mentioned in this chapter are:

Bevan, N. (1981)
Is there an optimum speed for presenting text on a VDU?
International Journal of Man-Machine Studies, 14, 59-76.

Duffy, T. (1985)
Preparing technical manuals: specification and guidelines.
In D. Jonassen (Ed) *The Technology of Text Vol. 2.*
Englewood Cliffs, NJ: Educational Technology Publications.

Foster, J.J. & Bruce, M. (1982)
Looking for entries in videotex tables: a comparison of four color formats.
Journal of Applied Psychology, 67, 5, 611-615.

Galitz, W.O. (1981)
Handbook of Screen Format Design.
Wellesley, Mass: QED Information Sciences.

Kolers, P., Duchnicky, R.L. & Ferguson, D.C. (1981)
Eye-movement measures of readability of CRT displays.
Human Factors, 23, 517-527.

Lancaster, F.W. & Warner, A. (1985)
Electronic publishing and its impact on the presentation of information.
In D. Jonassen (Ed) *The Technology of Text Vol. 2.*
Englewood Cliffs, NJ: Educational Technology Publications.

Reynolds, L. (1980)
Teletext and viewdata – a new challenge for the designer.
In J. Hartley (Ed) *The Psychology of Written Communication: Selected Readings.*
London: Kogan Page/New York: Nichols.

Simcox, W.A. (1983)
A framework for the inclusion of human factors in the design of videotex systems.
Information Design Journal, 3, 3, 215-230.

Wilkins, A.J. (1984)
Visual illusions, eye-strain, headaches and epilepsy.
Paper to the Annual meeting of The British Association for the Advancement of Science, September.
(Copies available from the author, MRC Applied Psychology Unit, 15 Chaucer Road, Cambridge CB2 2EF.)

Some useful articles are as follows:

Bork, A. (1983)
A preliminary taxonomy of ways of displaying text on screens.
Information Design Journal, 3, 3, 206-214.

Muter, P., Latremouille, S.A. & Treurniet, W.C. (1982)
Extended reading of continuous text on television screens.
Human Factors, 24, 5, 501-508.

Norrish, P. (1984)
Moving tables from paper to screen.
Visible Language, XVIII, 2, 154-170.

Reynolds, L., Spencer, H. & Glaze, G. (1978)
The legibility and readability of viewdata displays: a survey of relevant research.
Readability of Print Research Unit. London: Royal College of Art.

Waern, Y. & Rollenhagen, C. (1983)
Reading text from visual display units.
International Journal of Man-Machine Studies, 18, 441-465.

Two papers on work with electronic journals are:

Pullinger, D.J. (1984)
The design and presentation of the computer human factors journal in the Blend system.
Visible Language, XVIII, 2, 171–185.

Shackel, B. (1982)
The Blend system: programme for the study of some electronic journals.
Ergonomics, 25, 269-284.

Technical articles on legibility factors with VDUs, scrolling, etc can be found in the journals *Human Factors, International Journal of Man-Machine Studies*, and *Information Design Journal*. These journals are useful source materials for research related to this chapter.

Chapter 15 The specific references mentioned in this chapter are:

Buckingham, B.R. (1931)
New data on the typography of textbooks.
In G.M. Whipple (Ed) *The Textbook in American Education*.
NSSE Thirtieth Yearbook, Bloomington, Illinois.

Hartley, J. (1981)
Eighty ways of improving instructional text.
IEEE Transactions on Professional Communication, PC-24, 1, 17-27.

Klare, G.R. (1976)
Judging readability.
Instructional Science, 5, 1, 55-61.

Tulley, M. & Farr, R. (1985)
The purpose of State level textbook adoption: what does the legislation reveal?
Journal of Research and Development in Education (in press)

Unesco (1959)
Primary School Textbooks: Preparation, Selection and Use.
Paris: Unesco.

Wright, P. (1979)
The quality control of document design.
Information Design Journal, 1, 1, 33-42.

Appendix

The references for the case-histories described in this chapter are:

Burnhill, P. *et al* (1975)
The typography of college prospectuses: a critique and a case history.
In L. Evans & J. Leedham (Eds) *Aspects of Educational Technology IX*.
London: Kogan Page.

Burnhill, P., Hartley, J. & Young, M. (1976)
Tables in text.
Applied Ergonomics, 7, 1, 13-18.

Hartley, J. (1982)
Designing instructional text.
In D. Jonassen (Ed) *The Technology of Text*.
Englewood Cliffs, NJ: Educational Technology Publications.

Hartley, J. & Burnhill, P. (1976)
Explorations in space: a critique of the typography of BPS publications.
Bulletin of the British Psychological Society, 29, 97-107.

Hartley, J. & Trueman, M. (1985)
A research strategy for text designers: the role of headings.
Instructional Science (in press).

Hartley, J., Williams, C. & Trueman, M. (1980)
Choosing textbooks: the readability factor.
Head Teachers Review, April, pp. 2-4.

Some useful articles and books related to certain aspects of this chapter are:

Harrison, C. (1980)
Readability in the Classroom.
Cambridge: Cambridge University Press.

Kirst, M. (1984)
Choosing textbooks: reflections of a State Board President.
American Education, Summer, 1984, pp. 18-23.

Pearce, D. (1982)
Textbook Production in Developing Countries: Some Problems of Preparation, Production and Distribution.
Paris: Unesco.

Rye, J. (1982)
Cloze Procedure and the Teaching of Reading.
London: Heinemann Educational.

Zimet, S.G. (1976)
Print and Prejudice.
London: Hodder and Stoughton.

Alternative views concerning evaluation may be found in:

Jones, B. *et al* (1984)
Principles of content-driven comprehension, instruction and assessment.
Chapter 12 of *Content-Driven Comprehension, Instruction and Assessment: A Model for Army Training Literature*.
Technical Report, Alexandria, VA: Army Research Institute.

Sless, D. (1981)
Learning and Visual Communication.
London: Croom Helm.

Wright, P. (1985)
Is evaluation a myth? Assessing text assessment procedures.
In D. Jonassen (Ed) *The Technology of Text Vol. 2.*
Englewood Cliffs, NJ: Educational Technology Publications.

Section 3.   Resource materials

I have found the following journals useful to scan for articles on typographic research and instructional design. (A much longer list of relevant resource materials is presented in *Information Design Journal*, Vol. 4, No. 1, 1984.)

Applied Ergonomics
Butterworth Scientific Publications Ltd,
Journals Division, Box 63, Westbury House, Bury Street,
Guildford GU2 5BH.

Behaviour and Information Technology
Taylor & Francis Ltd,
4 John Street, London WC1N 2ET.

Educational Communication and Technology Journal
Association for Educational Communications and Technology,
1126 16th Street NW, Washington, DC 20036, USA.

Ergonomics
Taylor & Francis Ltd,
4 John Street, London WC1N 2ET.

Human Factors
Human Factors Society,
PO Box 1369, Santa Monica, California 90406, USA.

IEEE Transactions on Professional Communication
Institute of Electrical and Electronic Engineers Inc,
345 E 47th Street, New York, NY 10017, USA.

The Indexer
The Society of Indexers,
7A Parker Street, Cambridge CB1 1JL.

Information Design Journal
PO Box 185, Milton Keynes MK7 6BL.

Instructional Science
Elsevier Scientific Publishing Co,
PO Box 211, 100 QAE, Amsterdam, The Netherlands.

International Journal of Man-Machine Studies
Academic Press Inc (London) Ltd,
Oval Road, London NW1 7DX.

Journal of Educational Psychology
American Psychological Association,
120 Seventeenth Street NW, Washington, DC 20086, USA.

Journal of Research Communication Studies
Elsevier Scientific Publishing Co,
PO Box 211, 100 QAR, Amsterdam, The Netherlands.

Plain English
Plain English Campaign,
131 College Road, Manchester M15 0AA.

Scholarly Publishing
University of Toronto Press, Toronto, M55 1A6, Canada.

Simply Stated
Document Design Center,
American Institutes for Research, 1055 Thomas Jefferson Street NW,
Washington, DC 20007, USA.

Visible Language
Box 1972, Cleveland Museum of Art, Cleveland, OH 44106, USA.

Written Communication
Sage Publications,
PO Box 5024, Beverly Hills, California 90210, or
28 Banner Street, London EC1Y 8QE.

Section 4. Titles of British and American Standards

National and international standard publications contain codes of practice which provide valuable information for printers, authors and designers.

The following selection of British Standards illustrates the variety available. (Further information can be obtained from the British Standards Institution, 2 Park Street, London W1A 2BS.)

Books, literature and references

BS 1413:1970   (1982) Page sizes for books.
BS 1629:1976   Recommendations for bibliographical references.
BS 1749:1969   Alphabetical arrangement and the filing order of numerals and symbols.
BS 2509:1970   (1977) Presentation of serial publications, including periodicals.
BS 3700:1976   (1983) Recommendations for the preparation of indexes to books, periodicals and other publications.
BS 4187:1973   Parts 1 and 3. Specification for microfiche.
BS 4446:1969   (1977) Presentation of conference proceedings.
BS 4605:1970   (1977) Presentation of library directories.
BS 4884:1974   Part 2. Specification for technical manuals presentation.
BS 5605:1978   Recommendations for citing publications by bibliographical reference.
BS 5641:1982   Recommendations for loose-leaf publications.

Paper and stationery

BS 1808	Sizes and recommended layouts of commercial forms.
BS 5537:1978	Specification for form design sheet and layout chart.
BS 4000:1983	Sizes of papers and boards.

Conversion factors, symbols and abbreviations

BS 1219:1958	Recommendations for preparation of mathematical copy and correction of mathematical proofs.
BS 1219M:1961	Preparation of mathematical copy and correction of proofs.
BS 4058:1973	(1980) Data-processing flow chart symbols, rules and conventions.
BS 5261	Copy preparation and proof correction: Part 1:1975. Recommendations for preparation of typescript for printing. Part 2:1976. Typographic requirements, marks for copy preparation and proof correction, proofing procedure.
BS 5261C:1976	Marks for copy preparation and proof correction.

Glossaries

BS 2961:1967	Typeface nomenclature and classification.
BS 3203:1979	Glossary of paper, board, pulp and related terms.
BS 3527:1976	Glossary of terms used in data-processing (nine parts).
BS 3814:1964	Glossary of letterpress rotary printing terms used in connection with newspaper, magazine and similar machines.
BS 4149:1967	(1979) Glossary of paper/ink terms for letterpress printing.
BS 4277:1968	(1979) Glossary of terms used in offset lithographic printing.
BS 4335:1972	Glossary of terms used in project network techniques.
BS 5408:1976	Glossary of documentation terms.

In addition to these standards, the British Standards Institute publishes *Guides for Teachers in Technical Education*. These guides list British Standards Institute education section publications, and are regularly updated. Standards of particular relevance to this text are:

PD 7300	Nuts and bolts: recommended drawing ratios for schools and colleges.
PD 7301	Graphical communication: a teacher's pack.
PD 7302	Compendium of British Standards for design and technology in schools.
PD 7307	Graphical symbols for use in schools and colleges.
PD 7308	Engineering drawing practice for schools and colleges.

American standards are published by the American National Standards Institute, 1430 Broadway, New York, NY 10018; Telephone (212) 354 300.

Internationally agreed standards are available from the International Standards Organization (ISO), 1 Rue de Varende, 1211 Geneva 20, Switzerland.

A catalogue listing both American and ISO standards is available from the American National Standards Institute.

Note: Relationships between American, British and international standards are not always in full agreement.

Section 5.   Sources of relevant research in the United Kingdom

Centre for Catalogue Research
Research into the use of bibliographic records in libraries for catalogues,
requisitions, issue systems, and resource sharing schemes. Some studies are
concerned with how the visual presentation of data affects usability.
Philip Bryant, Centre for Catalogue Research, University of Bath, Claverton
Down, Bath BA2 7AY.

Centre for Research on User Studies
Users' needs and behaviour in the design and operation of library and
information systems of all kinds. Information, advice, training and research.
Brian Clifford, Centre for Research on User Studies,
University of Sheffield, Sheffield S10 2JN.

Centre for the Study of Human Learning
Work with reading recorders to look at relationships between readers and
text.
LF Thomas, Centre for the Study of Human Learning,
Brunel University, Kingston Lane, Uxbridge, Middlesex UB8 3PH.

Clear Communication Associates Ltd
Work on the design and evaluation of forms, tables, manuals and
computer-based training.
Gill Scott, 48 Rochester Place, London NW1 9JT.

Coventry Polytechnic
Work on the presentation of videotex, electronic graphics, and low-cost
printing technologies for the Third World.
Ian McLaren, Department of Graphic Design, Coventry (Lanchester)
Polytechnic, Gosford Street, Coventry CV1 5RZ.

Department of Chemistry, University of Glasgow
Work on the simplification of examination questions, and on the redesign of
lecture handouts and worksheets for laboratory classes.
Alex H Johnstone, Chemistry Department, The University, Glasgow
G12 8QQ.

Department of Human Sciences, Loughborough University
Work on various aspects of electronic journals – writing, editing, refereeing,
presentation, reading, skimming.
Brian Shackel, Department of Human Sciences, Loughborough University of
Technology, Loughborough, Leicestershire LE11 3TU.

Department of Psychology, University of Keele
Work on the layout and the writing of instructional text.
James Hartley, Department of Psychology, University of Keele, Keele,
Staffordshire ST5 5BG.

Department of Psychology, Manchester Polytechnic
Work on reading videotex CRT displays and the design of forms.
JJ Foster, Department of Psychology, Manchester Polytechnic, Elizabeth
Gaskell Building, Hathersage Road, Manchester M13 0JA.

Appendix

Department of Typography and Graphic Communication, University of Reading
Typographic analysis of documents, linguistic aspects of typography, form design, the history of printing, typographic design on screens. The department houses the Otto and Marie Neurath Collection (the archives of the former Isotype Institute Ltd) and runs a Forms Information Centre, which acts as an information and resources centre for the writing and design of forms.
Michael Twyman, Department of Typography & Graphic Communication, University of Reading, Whiteknights, Reading RG6 2AU.

Ergonomics Development Unit, University of Aston
Research on computer-based instruction and human-computer interface design.
Rob Stammers, Ergonomics Development Unit, University of Aston, Kyrle Hall, Gosta Green, Birmingham B4 7ET.

Ergonomics Research Group, University of Hull
In the area of information systems and design the group is currently working on the use and comprehension of heating controls in domestic central heating systems and the design of bus maps and timetables.
David Bartram, Ergonomics Research Group, University of Hull, 26 Newland Park, Hull HU5 2DW.

Ergonomics Unit, University of London
Work on factors affecting the comprehension of text – especially used in the course of human-computer interaction. Also, factors affecting second language speakers' comprehension of text.
John Long, Ergonomics Unit, University College London, 26 Bedford Way, London WC1H 0AP.

Graphic Information Research Unit, Royal College of Art
This Unit has now ceased to function, but papers on its work are available. Work was carried out on the legibility of alternative letter shapes, the effects of variations of in-set width on the legibility of text, typographic coding in bibliographic materials, the effects of degradation (through, for example, repeated copying) on the legibility of print, computer-generated alphanumeric characters, the effects of different kinds of background 'noise' on the legibility of print, the design of microform information and directional signing in museums and libraries.
Linda Reynolds, Royal College of Art, 6A Cromwell Place, London SW7 2NJ.

Information Technology Programme, Open University
Work on the design of Open University distance-learning texts, on forms, instructions, tabular and diagrammatic presentations, readability of text, content analysis of texts, structures of knowledge, ways in which learners interact with text. Research on screen-based systems, including expert aids to the design of tables and forms.
Paul Lefrere, Institute of Educational Technology, Open University, Milton Keynes, Buckinghamshire MK7 6AA.

Medical Research Council, Applied Psychology Unit, Cambridge
Tabular presentation of materials, the design of forms, instructions etc, flow charts and algorithms, display factors associated with entering alphanumeric codes on forms and with remembering them, reading skills.
Patricia Wright, MRC Applied Psychology Unit, 15 Chaucer Road, Cambridge CB2 2EF.

Plain English Campaign, Stockport
Publishes newsheets *Plain English*, language and layout of forms, runs training courses, advises on and conducts research on all aspects of plain English.
Chrissie Maher, Plain English Campaign, Vernon House, Whaley Bridge, Stockport ST12 7HP.

Primary Communications Research Centre
Work on all aspects of primary communications – ie scientific journals – in particular on how people acquire information when browsing, and cost factors in electronic publishing.
AJ Meadows, Primary Communications Research Centre, University of Leicester, Leicestershire LE1 7RH.

Royal Air Force Institute of Aviation
Work on the design and evaluation of maps and of displays of tabular alphanumeric data.
V David Hopkin, Royal Air Force Institute of Aviation Medicine, Farnborough, Hampshire GU14 6SZ.

Section 6. Sources of relevant research in the USA and Canada

The American Educational Research Association contains three relevant special interest groups. These are Research in Writing Skills; Textbooks, Textbook Publishing and Schools; and Text Design and Learner Strategies.
AERA, 1230 17th St, NW, Washington, DC 20136.

AT&T Bell Laboratories, Murray Hill
Experimental and theoretical studies of reading; analysis of text effectiveness including affective impact; computer analysis of performance-relevant text features; individual style patterns in eye movements during reading; fundamental learning studies; instructional theories; individual differences in learning and cognition; quality control with procedural and instructional documents; context effects in learning and training.
Ernst Z Rothkopf, Head, Learning and Instruction Research Department, AT&T Bell Laboratories, 600 Mountain Avenue, Murray Hill, New Jersey 07974.

AT&T Bell Laboratories, Summit
The Human Performance Engineering Department of AT&T Bell Laboratories includes two groups doing work relevant to document design. The Document Technologies group has been responsible for the development and testing of computer-based language analysis programs like the UNIX Writer's Workbench Software; and the Documentation Systems groups have been responsible for the design and creation of UNIX system documentation as well as the development of document evaluation techniques. Both groups are concerned with computer-aided reading and writing.
Lawrence Frase, AT&T Bell Laboratories, River Road, Summit, New Jersey 07901.

Appendix

Carnegie-Mellon University
Research in the English Department is focused on modelling (1) reading processes, especially the strategic processes people bring to complex texts, and (2) writing processes. Currently the focus is on revision – how writers detect and diagnose problems in texts and the strategies that experts and novices bring to revising.
An (overlapping) centre is the Communication Design Center which does more applied research in the design of documents, especially computer manuals. It has pioneered the use of Protocol-Aided Revision in producing certifiably readable computer manuals.
Linda Flower, Department of English, Carnegie-Mellon University, Pittsburgh, Pennsylvania, PA 15213.

Chicago Public Schools
Develops instructional materials for teachers and students in elementary grades for three large-scale projects. R&D Team has applied text design research to develop innovative graphics and glossary texts, as well as considerate instructional texts and 'summary' texts in specific content area subjects.
Beau Fly Jones, North Central Regional Educational Laboratory, 295 Emroy Avenue, Elmhurst, Illinois 60126.

Department of the Army, US Army Research Institute
The Learning Technology Team pursues a program of research to improve cognitive skills embedded within existing training contexts, ie the design of instructional text, videodisc and computer-assisted instruction.
Specific cognitive skills targeted are: reading comprehension, interpretation of written orders, spatial/orientation skills, problem solving and decision making.
Richard P Kern, Department of the Army, US Army Research Institute, 5001 Eisenhower Avenue, Alexandria, Virginia 22333.

Document Design Center
The Document Design Center publishes *Simply Stated* and *Simply Stated in Business* – monthly newsletters which describe and list ongoing activities in the US. The Center also conducts and reports on research.
Robbin Battison, Document Design Center, American Institutes for Research, 1055 Thomas Jefferson Street, NW, Washington, DC 20007.

Educational Products Information Exchange (EPIE) Institute
The EPIE Institute is a non-profit research and development organization which is devoted to providing evaluations and information on instructional materials to educators. EPIE evaluates textbooks and microcomputer educational software in major elementary and secondary curriculum areas. It also provides this information via electronic database and publishes a number of newsletters.
Arthur Woodward, EPIE Institute, PO Box 839, Water Mill, NY 11976.

McGill University
Research on elementary and secondary students' comprehension of different types of fictional and expository text (in particular, science texts); research on cognitive processes in discourse production and the relationship of discourse production to comprehension; studies of inferential processes in comprehending and integrating knowledge acquired from texts and other sources.
Carl H Fredericksen, Department of Educational Psychology and Counselling, Faculty of Education, McGill University, 3700 McTavish Street, Montreal, PQ, Canada H3A 1Y2.

Ohio University
The Department of Psychology has research interests in cognitive processes in writing, reading and studying; and special interests in the readability and comprehensibility of written materials. There is also interdisciplinary research with faculty members in the Department of English and the School of Journalism.
George Klare, Office of the Dean, College of Arts and Sciences, Ohio University, Athens, Ohio 45701.

Online Computer Library Center Inc
The Center designed and operates a bibliographic computer and telecommunications system that supports resource sharing among libraries. Current areas of investigation include: distributed processing, electronic document delivery, human-computer interaction, improved access techniques, microcomputer applications, and online catalogues.
Michael J McGill, Director for Technical Planning, Online Computer Library Center Inc, 6565 Frantz Road, Dublin, Ohio 43017.

University of Georgia
At the University of Georgia there is an interdisciplinary program of research on the design and comprehension of expository text. The University also serves as the base for the Text Design and Learner Strategies Special Interest Group of the American Educational Research Association.
Shawn Glynn, Department of Educational Psychology, Research and Measurement, University of Georgia, Athens, Georgia 30602.

University of North Carolina
Investigations into the instructional design display of text and textual features with a recent emphasis on the application of those principles to the design of microcomputer course work and concept mapping.
D Jonassen, School of Education, University of North Carolina at Greensboro, Greensboro, North Carolina 27412.

University of Minnesota
Programs in composition and communication – especially computer-aided writing.
Donald Ross and Lillian Bridwell, Principal Investigators, Program in Composition and Communication, University of Minnesota, Minneapolis, MN 55455.

US Navy Personnel-Research Center
Research on readability and design of instructional text, computer-based instructional manuals, document and display design.
William B Montague, Senior Scientist, Training Laboratory, Navy Personnel Research and Development Center, San Diego, CA 92152.

Westinghouse Corporation
Work on a computer-aided editing system called WRITEAIDS. The system analyses technical writing and automatically suggests changes for improving writing readability and comprehensibility. Work on automated page layout of text/graphic instructional materials.
J Douglas Kniffin, Defense and Electronic Systems Center, Westinghouse Corporation, 20 Corporate Center, 10400 Little Patuxent Parkway, Columbia, Maryland 21044.

Subject index

Author index